THE *Bluffer's*® GUIDE TO

POETRY

Nick Yapp

Edited by
Richard Meier

Colette House
52-55 Piccadilly
London W1J 0DX
United Kingdom

Email: info@bluffers.com
Website: bluffers.com
Twitter: @BluffersGuide

First published 1989
This edition published 2013
Copyright © Bluffer's® 2013

Publisher: Thomas Drewry
Publishing Director: Brooke McDonald

Series Editor: David Allsop
Design and Illustration: Jim Shannon

A CIP Catalogue record for this book
is available from the British Library.

Bluffer's Guide®, Bluffer's® and Bluff Your Way®
are registered trademarks.

ISBN: 978-1-909365-36-0 (print)
      978-1-909365-37-7 (ePub)
      978-1-909365-38-4 (Kindle)

CONTENTS

Poetry is 'the spontaneous overflow of powerful emotions recollected in tranquillity'. Put another way, more mathematically if you like: emotion + time elapsed = poetry. Emotion + immediate outpouring = tweet.

THE SPONTANEOUS OVERFLOW

WHAT IS POETRY?

In the days when typesetting was still done by hefty blokes arranging small pieces of lead in a wooden box, pretty much everything on paper that looked neatly aligned on the left and a raggedy mess on the right could be considered poetry. Now that we're all dab hands at document layout, such certainty has long evaporated and a more complicated definition is needed. It's really a question of discovering what Donne, Anon, ee cummings, Ovid, Pam Ayres and Percy Bysshe Shelley have in common; or what connects *The Epic of Gilgamesh,* greetings card verses, naughty limericks, 'Ode to a Nightingale', 'Sing a Song of Sixpence' and *Paradise Lost.*

To do this, the biggest mistake is to look at the end products themselves. There appear to be no similarities whatsoever between a Shakespearean sonnet and a Matsuyaman haiku, between a Milligan couplet and three or four thousand lines of Alexander Pope, between one of Edward Lear's nonsense rhymes and the neo-futuristic monologues of Andrei Voznesensky.

Note: Don't worry if a lot of words like 'neo-futuristic', 'polemical', 'panegyric', 'iconoclastic', etc. mean nothing to you. Just use them in a slightly haughty manner before anyone else does, and then add: 'Not a word that one would normally think of applying to his (or her) verse, perhaps...'

This book concentrates on English poetry, with a nod towards the USA and the wider world. Even so, somewhere, someday, someone will hurl a name at you that you don't recognise, a balladeer of whom you know nothing. This is when you should smile enigmatically, and fall back on one of the following bluffs:

a) 'Yes, I suppose it's about time I rediscovered him (or her).' This implies that you were aware of this poet ages ago, practically before the ink (or blood) dried on the manuscript. Equally, you might say: 'Yes, I suppose it's about time I rediscovered his (or her) work.' Poetry buffs never refer to poems, only to the poet's work. This may or may not be because they have never done any in their lives and don't know what real work is.

b) 'Too deceptive for me, I'm afraid.' This implies that you have seen through the poet's deception, whereas your companion hasn't.

c) 'I'm afraid that my approach to him (her) can only be described as lacklustre.' Although you are ostensibly criticising yourself, the implication is that the poet is hardly worth considering.

You can rediscover anybody – Byron, Ogden Nash,

Banjo Paterson, even Gertrude Stein ('Rose is a rose is a rose is a rose'). Here you are using a Compound Bluff technique, suggesting that not only have you known the poet's work since infancy but that you are constantly re-evaluating poetry, seeking (and finding) new levels of appreciation, new depths of meaning.

'Depths of meaning' is what poetry is all about. All poetry is deep, profound, heavy, bottomless, suffocating, unfathomable. If you can understand it, it isn't poetry – it's verse. And then your appreciation should draw on the language of the wine expert. Verse is 'crisp and dry' like a white Burgundy, or 'sparkling and clear' like a young Champagne. Verse can be about anything. Poetry concerns itself only with the inexorable course of love, rejection and death, although a great many poets don't bother too much with the first two, but hasten to the last.

Poetry is what happens when sensitive people find themselves overcome and have pen and paper (or tablet) to hand. They may be overcome by all sorts of emotions or feelings: love, joy (rare), despair (every day), wonderment (often faked), death wish (enormously common), horror, patriotism (outmoded), faith, lust (but only in a caring sort of way) – the list is endless. The source of the emotion may be almost anything: the Bible, a battle, a daffodil, a woman, a man, a bird, sunsets, the smell of frying onions. The reaction is always the same. Out come pen and paper, down goes the poem.

Other types of writer don't say: 'I wrote this novel when I was walking along Hadrian's Wall' or 'One night, when

I was swimming the Hellespont, I simply had to write this play'. Poets do. The outcome of their jottings may be very long or very short. The works may or may not rhyme. They may or may not scan (*see* 'Glossary'). It doesn't matter. Because they are verbal responses to surfeits of emotion; they are poetry. Whether or not they are good poetry is, of course, another matter. Poetry, as Wordsworth so succinctly put it, is 'the spontaneous overflow of powerful emotions recollected in tranquillity'. Put another way, more mathematically if you like: emotion + time elapsed = poetry. Emotion + immediate outpouring = tweet.

POETS AS BLUFFERS

400 years ago, Sir Philip Sidney (poet, wit, scholar, soldier, courtier and gent) wrote: 'Now for the poet, he nothing affirmeth, and therefore never lieth.'

It's an interesting line for two reasons. Firstly, it shows that even in those days poets were using archaic English – 'thees' and 'thous' and 'listeth' and 'lieth'.

Secondly, brave hero and jolly good chap though he may have been, Sir Philip was also a consummate bluffer. Poets are inveterate liars, constantly bending and breaking rules and ignoring Truth for the sake of Art.

Rupert Brooke was one of the worst offenders. Thousands can quote from his poem 'The Old Vicarage, Grantchester'; it's one of the Good Old Good Ones of English Verse:

Stands the church clock at ten to three?
And is there honey still for tea?

The church clock did stick in Grantchester in 1911, but at half past three, not 10 to three. Why the change? Half past three rhymes; it even scans as well. Either Rupert Brooke couldn't wait for his tea, or he simply wanted to bluff for the sake of bluffing. It's a common practice in verse and is known as 'poetic licence' – granting poets a special station not accorded anyone else. A street trader's licence doesn't legitimise untruths or malpractices on the trader's part.

♛

> Poetic licence allows any
> and every poet to indulge in regular
> bouts of bluffing.

A publican's licence doesn't permit him to water his beer (*see* GK Chesterton, 'Other Schools to Know About', page 84) or falsify the labels on his bottles. A driving licence is not a passport to deceit. But poetic licence allows any and every poet to indulge in regular bouts of bluffing. Not that poets have always had it their own way, however. Plato, for example, saw through them and their ways, and banished the whole lying lot of them from his imaginary republic. Sensible chap.

One of the most egregious manifestations of poetic mendacity goes by the name of the 'pathetic fallacy'. This is a literary device where a poet will attribute a human emotion (usually his own) to some inanimate object or other (often, but not exclusively, an aspect of the natural world, such as a landscape). This bit is the fallacy. Poetry buffs will tell you that the pathetic part refers to the pathos or empathy required by the poet to pull off this feat. Others might argue that it's called pathetic because describing, say, a Welsh dresser or a Bognor Regis beachscape as, for example, sad, is, well, sad.

And the porkies don't stop at the composition of poetry. As a young poet, John Clare used to recite his work to groups at markets and fairs. They laughed at his poems until, as he explains, he 'hit upon a harmless deception by repeating my poems over a book as though I was reading it. This had the desired effect. They often praised them and said if I could write as good, I should do.' This, you should maintain, is why poets, above all others, are prepared to pay to see their work in print.

Other examples of bluffing are scattered throughout this slim volume. Take the whole convention of the pastoral – the independent, cheerful, hardy, virtuous peasant, hugely enjoying a life of poverty-stricken, back-breaking grind in a mixture of appalling weathers – which is just one enormous poetic bluff, delivered by Burns, Clare, Wordsworth and Duck (among others). And Newbolt, Tennyson, Kipling and the Patriotic Poets of the nineteenth century were wildly inaccurate in their depictions of historical events.

Having considered all of this, there might still be a question niggling at the back of your mind about the precise purpose of a guide such as this. After all, why would anybody want to bluff about an arcane literary genre which began when primitive man first picked up a piece of flint and gouged a rudimentary ode on a cave wall – and effectively ended when Paul McCartney wrote the memorable words: 'But if this ever-changing world in which we live in…' (Yes, it was a song lyric – but it's much the same sort of thing – *see* 'American Poetry and Some of the Rest').

As a literary art form, poetry has surely had its ups and downs, but for anyone wishing to state their literary credentials, a passing knowledge of poems and poets is vital. You don't need to know why; you just need to know.

This book sets out to guide you through the main danger zones encountered in poetry discussions, and to equip you with a vocabulary and an evasive technique that will minimise the risk of being rumbled as a bluffer. It will give you a few easy-to-learn hints and methods that will allow you to be accepted as a poetry aficionado of rare ability and experience. But it will do more. It will give you the tools to impress legions of marvelling listeners with your knowledge and insight – without anyone discovering that you don't actually know the difference between a *leitmotif* and a limerick. As far as the former is concerned, look no further than the war poet Edmund Blunden's words in his 1917 poem 'Pillbox':

Come, Bluffer, where's your wits?

When entering a competition,
send in a totally inappropriate poem.
That way you can trumpet your lack
of success to the poetry community
by saying that 'the Philistines' didn't
have the guts to consider your stuff.

POETRY BASICS

For some people, Poetry is Life. They buy books of poetry; they go to poetry readings and performances; they go to poetry clubs and societies; they write the stuff and pay to get it published; they care and worry and fuss about poetry.

These are the Poetry Fanatics and you must beware of them. If you live in certain parts of London, the lusher suburbs of other cities, or towns with literary connections or festivals (Cheltenham, Hay-on-Wye and Aldeburgh, for example), you may find them hard to avoid. They're in the mould of the Ancient Mariner – mad eyes staring, dribble coming out of the corners of their mouths, seeking some poor wretch to whom they can recite at length. If you can't avoid them, you may consider joining them.

HOW TO DRESS FOR POETRY

Don't:

- Wear a velvet smoking jacket or thick cord trousers; people will think you're a psychotherapist.

- Grow a beard. No great poet of the last 100 years or so has sported a beard. Okay, Ginsberg had a real faceful but you might challenge anyone on this point by observing that a great big beard doth not a great poet make.

- Slap on a beret. People will think you're from the Royal British Legion or the local farmers' market.

- Wear sandals. People will think you couldn't afford a decent pair of trainers.

- Drip around in a silk dressing gown. People will think you're emulating Ivor Novello or Noël Coward.

Do:

- Roll your own cigarettes, as messily as possible, if you happen to smoke.

- Kit yourself out in a Panama hat, white linen jacket, and two-tone brogues. People won't know which poet you evoke, and that will disturb them.

- Whatever you do, though, you must ensure that nothing that you wear matches. Poets are renowned for their heightened powers of observation but this faculty must absolutely not extend to noticing that one's lime-green chinos clash rather garishly when coupled with that favourite, and seldom-washed, puce cardie.

HOW TO TREAT POETRY BOOKS

The moment you buy a book of verse, mutilate it:

- Break the spine.

- Fold down the corners as though marking pages.

- Spill some dark brown (or, better, Burgundian red) liquid on it.

- Tear out a few pages.

- Scribble dates and obtuse references in the margins.

Most people who buy poetry books never even open them, let alone read them, so when you turn up with a volume that looks as though London Wasps have been playing with it, you will be regarded with awe.

WHAT TO DO WHEN SOMEONE THREATENS YOU WITH A POEM THEY'VE WRITTEN

The vital thing is to prevent them reading it to you. If they do, you have to try to listen and then make a comment. So, when they say: 'May I read you my latest oeuvre?', firmly respond: 'No. Don't do that. I've just spent three days and nights reading The New Apocalyptics and my mind is completely shattered. Do you know The New Apocalyptics, by any chance ?' They won't.

HOW TO BEHAVE AT POETRY READINGS

Two or three decades ago, when performance poetry was in its heyday, one could turn up, quite innocently, at the Royal

Festival Hall, the Barbican or any large theatre, hoping for some foot-tapping, lightweight, free entertainment while you guzzle real ale, and find two men (it was always two men) shouting bits of verse at each other and making strange and obscene noises into handheld microphones.

Unless you are an attendant social worker or conducting important research into egomaniacal behaviours, you must simply leave at once.

These days, the poetry 'slam' is the thing. If you have the misfortune to stumble upon one of these events where very unshy 'poets' vie with each other to declaim their right-on, self-referential tosh, there are two strategies open to you:

1. Run away and drink elsewhere.

2. Wait until they appear to have ground to a halt (it may take a very long time), then trot over to them and say how much you enjoyed it and could they please do something of Eleanor Farjeon's?

Even when the entertainment on offer is of the more traditional poet-mumbles-a-few-poems-from-his-slim-book-interspersed-with-interminable-explanations-of-the-arcane-references-he-put-in-said-poems-to-make-himself-appear-more-interesting-than-he-really-is variety, the organisers of such events will more often than not devote some portion of the proceedings to an 'open-mic' (pronounced 'mike') section. This is where anyone with a mild-to-moderate mental-health problem will get up from the audience and spout a truly terrible and incomprehensible bit of drivel which has been repeatedly rejected by editors of poetry magazines up and down the land.

In this case – unless you are an attendant social worker or conducting important research into egomaniacal behaviours – you must simply leave at once.

POETRY COMPETITIONS

There are an enormous number of these, organised both nationally and locally. The Poetry Library at London's Southbank Centre has a comprehensive list but it's no good entering any of them as every poetry competition has about 2 million submissions, even if the first prize is less than a fiver (it usually is). Very often the entries are sifted by an undergraduate student who is currently enrolled in the creative writing course on which the poet-cum-adjudicator is a teacher, and thus only a handful or so of the poems entered ever pass in front of the big cheese poet supposedly judging the prize.

If you feel you must take part, however, here are a few pointers to increase your chances of success: ensure that the poems you enter are between 16 and 24 lines long. No poem shorter or longer than this ever wins a poetry competition:

any shorter and the adjudicators will be scared that the entrants might think they couldn't be bothered to read the medium-length ones; any longer and the adjudicators, who will have thousands of entries to wade through, will never read it to the end.

Alternatively, send in a totally inappropriate poem (obscene or blasphemous if it's your local paper; coyly sentimental or nauseatingly anthropomorphic if it's The Poetry Society). That way you can trumpet your lack of success to the poetry community by saying that 'the Philistines' didn't have the guts to consider your stuff. A word of warning, though: don't submit a coyly sentimental or nauseatingly anthropomorphic poem to The Spectator poetry competition. You may just win it. Better to enter a paean to the Labour Party or the union block vote (which will give you no chance). And make sure there is not a single rhyme.

ANTHOLOGIES

Never admit to having bought any of the general anthologies of verse (The Oxford Book of English Verse, The Faber Book of English Verse, Palgrave's Golden Treasury, The Reader's Digest Book of Rhymes, etc.). Be sneering in your approach to them ('One up from Poems for Children Under Nine, perhaps…'). Reserve maximum levels of dismissiveness for the slew of self-help anthologies that now exist with faux-dramatic titles such as Poems You Need to Make It through the Morning and Poems You Absolutely Need to Read Because this World is Very Cruel and Not at all Fair, aimed at convincing the troubled and faintly narcissistic poetry lover that this particular tome (and they are always tomes – who ever heard of a short anthology?) will solve all their woes.

In addition to these, there are hundreds of different sorts of anthologies, and the bluffer should go full tilt for the most unlikely (*French Cowherd Songs, Burmese Love Poetry, CND Battle Cries, Boardroom Ballads,* etc.). However, such is the proliferation of anthologies these days that you may find that your chosen bluff does in fact already exist (if you think this is a far-fetched claim, check out *Poetry of the Taliban* ('Decapitation: An Ode', anyone?), or *There's Rosemary:* 'An Anthology of Poetry, Published By The Monmouthshire Education Committee in 1969, the Year of the Investiture of the Prince of Wales').

The only other way to use anthologies to your advantage is to make a careful note of the compiler and the date of publication. If you talk of Stallworthy's 1973 *Compilation of Love Poetry,* Hadfield's *Sea Verse* for Chameleon Books in 1940, or Weissbort's *Post-war Russian Poetry* for Penguin in 1974, you will be exhibiting knowledge that no one else possesses, which to many poetry buffs (not bluffs) is the Essence of Life.

It doesn't matter how obscure the anthology is; in fact, the more obscure the better. *A Third Ladybird Book of Nursery Rhymes* may be the only book of poetry you possess, but if you refer to it as *Wills & Hepworth's Folk Verse Anthology* ('1962, wasn't it, or '63?'), people can't help but be impressed.

UNDERSTANDING THE VOCABULARY

Bluffers should realise that poets not only find spelling difficult, they also use words and phrases that the rest of us don't. Here are a few, with translations:

Fain would I I'd like to, but I really don't think I can

Lo! I say! (or) Wow!

Muse I say! (or) Wow!

Behold Look

Ah! Oh!

Sith Since

Bootes Avails

Avails Benefits

Methought It occurred to me...

Roseate Pinkish

Hark! Please pay attention!

Goodly Dull

Plentious In stock, available

Such an one One of them

Doubt you? You sayin' I'm lyin'?

Alas! Oh dear

Hoarie Freezing

For the nonce   While I'm waiting...

Bosome   Chest, lap, hill, sea bed, schooldays, heaven – anything but breast.

The poetic vocabulary also includes thee, thou, thereto, thy, doth, ye, commeth, whiles, twixt, makyth, fayrest, unto, eeke, begot, wilt, e'en, ere and heaps of other words whose meaning is nearly obvious; and certain constructions, such as 'much was I', 'quoth he', 'twas so', 'your trumpets sound'. Most of these constructions stem from an understandable desire on the part of the poet to end the line with an easy rhyme; it's much easier to find a rhyme for 'so' than 'twas', for 'sound' than 'trumpets'.

The other philological vagary of poets is that they find it impossible to make other than classical allusions to certain objects – the sun is always 'Phoebus'; the nightingale, 'Philomel'; a canine, 'Cerberus'; heaven, 'Elysium'; a wedding, 'Hymen'; a tease, 'Nymphe' or 'Nimph'.

You just have to get used to all of this.

The safest foundation for the bluffer in poetry is to have full knowledge of what most people can merely recollect hazily.

FAMOUS SHORT VERSES

U nless you wish to aim very high indeed, the safest
foundation for the bluffer in poetry is to have full
knowledge of what most people can merely recollect
hazily. Here, the couplet – two lines of verse that frequently
rhyme – is your friend. And so is anything of four lines or
under (or even more in the case of Wordsworth's estimable
'The Rainbow') To this end, commit the following 20
snatches of verse (or as many of them as you can) to
memory, remember where they came from and who wrote
them, and use them at every opportunity. NB: the secret in
most cases is to know the second line.

1. *'Beauty is truth, truth beauty,' – that is all*
   Ye know on earth, and all ye need to know.
   'Ode on a Grecian Urn', John Keats

2. *The boy stood on the burning deck*
   Whence all but he had fled;
   The flame that lit the battle's wreck
   Shone round him o'er the dead.
   'Casabianca', Felicia Dorothea Hemans

3. *I grow old…I grow old…*
   I shall wear the bottoms of my trousers rolled.
   'The Love Song of J Alfred Prufrock', TS Eliot

4. *Oh, East is East and West is West, and never the*
   twain shall meet,
   Till Earth and Sky stand presently at God's great
   Judgement Seat.
   'The Ballad of East and West', Rudyard Kipling

5. *– O what made fatuous sunbeams toil*
   To break earth's sleep at all?
   'Futility', Wilfred Owen

6. *Come live with me and be my love,*
   And we will all the pleasures prove.
   'The Passionate Shepherd to His Love', Christopher Marlowe

7. *Not in vain the distance beacons. Forward, forward*
   let us range,
   Let the great world spin for ever down the ringing
   grooves of change.
   'Locksley Hall', Alfred, Lord Tennyson

8. *Golden slumbers kiss your eyes,*
   Smiles awake you when you rise.
   'Golden Slumbers' (and borrowed by The Beatles for 'Golden Slumbers', *Abbey Road*), Thomas Dekker

9. *Here a little child I stand,*
   Heaving up my either hand.

'A Child's Grace', Robert Herrick

10. *But soon a wonder came to light,*
    That showed the rogues they lied:
    The man recovered of the bite,
    The dog it was that died.
    'An Elegy on the Death of a Mad Dog',
    Oliver Goldsmith (NB: the secret here
    is to remember the first line.)

11. *To see a world in a grain of sand,*
    And a heaven in a wild flower,
    Hold infinity in the palm of your hand,
    And eternity in an hour.
    'Auguries of Innocence', William Blake

12. *Wee, sleekit, cow'rin, tim'rous beastie,*
    O, what a panic's in thy breastie!
    'To a Mouse, on Turning Her Up in her Nest with
    the Plough, November, 1785', Robert Burns
    (NB: the secret here is to try to remember what must
    be the longest title of any poem.)

13. *My heart leaps up when I behold*
    A rainbow in the sky:
    So was it when my life began;
    So is it now I am a man;
    So be it when I shall grow old,
    Or let me die!
    The child is father of the man;
    And I could wish my days to be

Bound each to each by natural piety.
'The Rainbow', William Wordsworth

14. *O, young Lochinvar is come out of the west,*
Through all the wide Border his steed was the best.
'Lochinvar', Sir Walter Scott

15. *The Assyrian came down like a wolf on the fold,*
And his cohorts were gleaming in purple and gold.
'The Destruction of Sennacherib', Lord Byron

16. *The trumpet of a prophecy! O Wind,*
If Winter comes, can Spring be far behind?
'Ode to the West Wind', Percy Bysshe Shelley

17. *I mount! I fly!*
O Grave! Where is thy victory?
O Death! Where is thy sting?
'The Dying Christian to his Soul', Alexander Pope

18. *Against the Brydale day, which was not long:*
Sweet Thames run softly, till I end my song.
'Prothalamion', Edmund Spenser

19. *Stands the church clock at ten to three?*
And is there honey still for tea?
'The Old Vicarage, Grantchester', Rupert Brooke

20. *Here with a Loaf of Bread beneath the Bough,*
A Flask of Wine, a Book of Verse – and Thou.
'The Rubaiyat of Omar Khayyam of Naishapur',
Edward FitzGerald

POETS AND DEATH

An enormous number of poets died strange, heroic or untimely deaths. It's hard to be rhapsodic about these; bluffers are caring people, who don't go around revelling in the fact that Marlowe, Fergusson, Chatterton, Shelley, Keats, Emily Brontë and many others all died at or before they were 30. Say instead what a pity it was that Tennyson, Wordsworth, Hardy, Belloc, de la Mare, Masefield and Graves lived so long. 'Think what they would have accomplished,' you can say, 'had their energies been concentrated, as Shelley's was, into two or three decades.' People won't understand and assume that you must have a point.

However, for those of a morbid disposition, here is a list of poets for whom Death cameth either soon rather than late, or in a particularly individual manner:

GUILLAUME APOLLINAIRE (1880-1918)

French Cubist poet (though believed to have been born in Rome). Real name Wilhelm Apollinaris de Kostrowitsky. Began writing poetry while in La Santé Prison in Paris, where he'd been sent following his involvement with two statuettes stolen from the Louvre museum and sold to Picasso, and the subsequent theft of the *Mona Lisa* (believed to have been carried out by his shady secretary). Died of wounds received in the First World War.

GEORGE GORDON, LORD BYRON (1788-1824)

The Great Romantic. Died of fever after he'd joined the Greek insurgents fighting for liberation from Ottoman rule.

THOMAS CHATTERTON (1752-1770)

The Boy Wonder. Or 'the marvellous Boy / The sleepless Soul that perished in his pride', as Wordsworth put it, clearly a fan of this child genius who spent most of his short life forging poems. Reduced to despair by his poverty (there's not much of a market for forged poems), he poisoned himself with arsenic – an image later captured by Pre-Raphaelite Henry Wallis in *The Death of Chatterton*.

JOHN CORNFORD (1915-1936)

Christened Rupert John after Rupert Brooke, who had just died and had been a friend of his parents. Academically brilliant and politically perceptive. Went to Spain and was killed by machine-gun fire the day after his 21st birthday. Read 'Full Moon At Tierz'.

FULKE GREVILLE, LORD BROOKE (1554-1628)

Murdered by his servant, Haywood, who thought himself omitted from his master's will. (This always seems such a silly crime – surely the time to murder someone is when you're included in their will.)

FEDERICO GARCÍA LORCA (1898-1936)
Spanish poet and playwright, murdered by the fascists early in the Spanish Civil War.

ROBIN HYDE (1906-1939)
Real name Iris Guiver Wilkinson. New Zealand poet who arrived ill in England after travelling through war-torn China, and soon committed suicide.

JOHN KEATS (1795-1821)
Possibly the most famous of the early departers. Died of consumption in Rome. Epitaph (written himself): 'Here lies one whose name was writ in water'.

CHRISTOPHER MARLOWE (1564-1593)
MI5's most famous poet, killed on active service in a pub in Deptford, ostensibly while arguing about the bill. His death shows:

a) Nobody should argue about the bill in Deptford.

b) You shouldn't mix poetry with espionage.

A lot of people think that Shakespeare's plays were written by Marlowe. But then again, apparently around 9 million Americans think they've been abducted by aliens.

CHARLOTTE MEW (1869-1928)

Following her sister's death, and frightened of loneliness and insanity, committed suicide.

SIR WALTER RALEIGH (1552-1618)

Unfairly tried on charge of plotting against James I, condemned to death, sent to the Tower from 1603 to 1616. Wrote some poems. Released to undertake an expedition to the Orinoco in search of gold. Failed to find any. Re-arrested on the demand of the Spanish ambassador, sent back to Tower, wrote more poems. Beheaded.

ROGER ROUGHTON (1916-1941)

Surrealist poet who killed himself in Dublin, but it may have been an accident – you can never tell with Surrealists.

PERCY BYSSHE SHELLEY (1792-1822)

Like Keats, made the mistake of moving to Italy and was drowned in the Bay of La Spezia while returning from visiting his friends Lord Byron and Leigh Hunt.

SIR PHILIP SIDNEY (1554-1586)

Joined in an attack on a Spanish convoy at Zutphen and received a fatal wound in the thigh.

ROBERT SOUTHEY (1774-1843)

Poet Laureate who died of softening of the brain. A desire to guard against this is probably the reason that so many aspiring poets affect floppy hats, berets, boaters, etc.

No one ever has a good word to say about his poetry these days, so a plea for critical leniency on account of his brain turning to mush is a sound bluff which will at once confer upon you both erudition and the possession of a compassionate nature.

HENRY HOWARD, EARL OF SURREY (1517-1547)

Executed for advising his sister to become Henry VIII's mistress, an arrangement that clearly didn't suit any of the three parties involved; the king himself a short while later. Escaped unpunished, however, for a much more heinous crime – introducing the sonnet to England (along with Wyatt – *see* 'From the Beginnings to the Bard', page 33).

ALGERNON SWINBURNE (1837-1909)

Born all but dead, wasn't expected to live an hour and was described by his contemporaries at Eton as a 'queer little elf' and 'a kind of fairy'. Peculiarly and congenitally unfit for dissipation, he gave it a try. Notorious for his interest in de Sade, his health prevented him from playing an active part. Died in Putney of pneumonia when the rest of the household went down with influenza.

JOHN WILMOT, EARL OF ROCHESTER (1647-1680)

Court wit and writer of shockingly lewd poems, 'blazed out his youth and health in lavish voluptuousness', and, quite simply, died of an excess.

Be warned: very few of Shakespeare's poems, or anybody else's for that matter, have happy endings.

FROM THE BEGINNINGS TO THE BARD

EARLY ORIGINS

Since nobody has the slightest idea where, when or why poetry began (i.e., who was the first to be overcome by the need to emote), this is a most fertile field for the bluffer. In poetry, the mists of obscurity lend a mellow fruitfulness to speculation, pretence and making very little knowledge go a very long way.

Of course, it's quite possible that one day an archaeologist digging away in the Lower Omo Valley, Ethiopia, will unearth a 30,000-year-old relic with a limerick carved on it, revealing an ape-like wit:

If ever they come to detect us,
They'll look at our skulls, and suspect us,
Of walking around
With our hands off the ground,
And label us Homo erectus.

Until then, our jumping-off point has to be the ancient city of Uruk in Mesopotamia.

About 4,000 years ago, a Sumerian poet prepared several

hundred clay tablets, sat down and then, in the wedge-shaped cuneiform writing of the day (which is tremendously easy to rhyme, when you come to look at it), wrote *The Epic of Gilgamesh*. This is a long poem about a king who was two parts god and one part man, who reigned for 126 years, and whose life was spent in a losing battle with what appears to be congenital pessimism – a very suitable subject for a poem. It's full of 'bitter weeping' and 'evil deeds' and 'was it for this I…' – the very stuff of poetry for millennia.

GLORIOUS GREEKS

1500 years later came the next great poem, Homer's *Iliad*, often described as the Bible of Greece. It isn't necessary to read it; just remember that it's about the the last days of the decade-long Trojan War, and go into raptures about how wonderful it must have been to hear it chanted by minstrels in the halls of kings – you can adopt this approach to all poetry composed before 1500 AD. The other thing to remember about the *Iliad*, and its sister poem the *Odyssey*, is that they are the only long narrative poems about deeds of valour that you shouldn't describe as 'Homeric'. If you must read one, try the *Odyssey*; it's 4,000 lines shorter.

Every four years, at the Panathenaea in Athens, Homer's epics were performed in front of a vast audience by 'rhapsodes' – men who carried long sticks and recited poems for a living. Perhaps they would have put on these performances with greater frequency had they not taken about three years and 11 months to get through them each time. If you really want to impress, you could espouse the cause of Hesiod, a lesser-known Greek poet, whose most famous piece was *Works and Days*, an 800-verse poem about a grumpy farmer – a bit like *The Archers*, but in dactylic hexameters (*see* 'Glossary').

ROMAN ROOTS

The father of Roman poetry was Ennius (c239-169 BC), who is alleged to have said: 'Unless I have the gout, I never write poetry'. In the end, of course, he died of both. Some consider Latin a terser, more forceful and more precise language than Greek, and say that the Roman poets (Virgil, Horace, Seneca, Propertius et al) displayed a constant moral concern and a more clinical attitude to the emotions. The upshot of all this is that Virgil's *Aeneid* is every bit as long as Homer's *Iliad* but you may, at least, describe the *Aeneid* as Homeric. Be careful: lots of people have heard of the *Aeneid*; fewer have heard of Virgil's other great work, *The Georgics*, which is about farming and the countryside. Bluffers will claim that the Cecil Day-Lewis translation is poetry itself.

If you wish to adopt a more saucy approach to poetry, let Ovid (43 BC-17 AD) be your Roman poet. A wordly individual, he wrote a great deal of naughty poetry and was eventually banished to Romania for his pains. His most famous works were the *Amores*, the *Heroides*, the *Ars Amatoria*, the *Tristia and Metamorphoses*. To show familiarity with his work, you don't have to read any of it: just smirk and roll your eyes a lot.

For those with a taste for the top shelf, Catullus is the Roman poet for you. Capable of out-smutting even the naughty boy Ovid, this poet is celebrated for a variety of lyrics including those to, and about, his beloved Lesbia, and others of supreme obscenity and invective. His poems, which do not have titles, are generally referred to by number; while this may initially seem a little odd – after all, untitled poems by other poets (Emily Dickinson, for example) are generally referred to by their opening lines – the fact that Catullus can open a poem with the charming 'Pedicabo ego vos et irrumabo' (I will sodomise you and face-f*** you) (Number 16) may explain this particular exception to the usual convention.

The most famous Roman poet of them all is Thomas Babington Macaulay (1800-1859 AD), who wrote the *Lays of Ancient Rome* (don't let all that Catullus stuff get you excited – 'lay' doesn't mean what you hope it does. *See* 'Glossary'). His poetry is wonderfully unfashionable now because it's tremendously easy to learn:

> *Then out spake brave Horatius,*
> *The Captain of the Gate:*
> *'To every man upon this earth*
> *Death cometh soon or late.'* ('Horatius')

EARLY ENGLISH

Always remember that English poetry (as, indeed, all European poetry) began life as ballads, songs and lays, recited by minstrels, troubadours and jongleurs to audiences of mead-quaffing monarchs and exhausted Irish wolfhounds.

The earliest English poetry that we know of is Northumbrian, but written in the language of Wessex. Poets clearly wished their work to be inaccessible even in those days. Many regard *Beowulf* (written by a Christian scribe around 700 AD) as the first English poem, but it was preceded by at least three others: *Widsith*, about Continental courts; *Waldhere*, about French heroism; and *The Fight at Finnesburgh*, which is yet another poem about a battle against fearful odds – the sort that Tennyson would have revelled in and which is bluff from beginning to end.

You can say what you like about these three poems; nobody's ever heard of them, let alone read them. Commit them to memory (the titles will suffice), then disregard anything that purports to be poetry until:

GEOFFREY CHAUCER (1343-1400)

Lots of people have heard of Chaucer because he and Shakespeare have long been the two compulsory English poets, so you have to be very careful here. Only recite a couple of the famous lines, written in Middle English, when you've practised the pronunciation (preferably with a slight West Country accent) as follows:

Hwann that Arrpril whith hiss sho-re sawta
the drochte of Maarge hath pair-sed to th' rota...

The important thing to remember about Chaucer is that his life remains largely a mystery. This gives great scope for bluffing. It is thought that he was employed in the Secret Service for a year, engaging in espionage in Flanders from

1376 to 1377, but there is uncertainty about when he was born, whom he married, and what he did for a living (nobody except Tennyson has ever written poetry for a living).

Since he travelled a great deal, you can speculate wildly about possible meetings he had with Boccaccio and Petrarch (the Italian poets), and talk earnestly (all poetry buffs are earnest) about Italian influences on his work ('…octosyllabic went right out of the proverbial window, never to return. Couple of glasses of Orvieto under the cypress with Petrarch and it was heroic stanzas all the way… seven lines a stanza…like the Seven Hills of Rome, d'you see?'). Proceed to describe his later phase ('…settled down in Aldgate and completely revamped his style…heroic couplets from then on…crowning achievement...try to imagine *The Canterbury Tales* in any other form…impossible.').

Don't dwell on *The Canterbury Tales*; it's too well known. Steer clear also of *Troilus and Criseyde* (you may invite a discussion on the merits and demerits of Chaucer's rendering versus Shakespeare's telling of the story). Talk instead about *The Book of the Duchess* ('Interesting but immature'), *The House of Fame* ('What a shame he never finished it') and *The Legend of Good Women* ('Which version of the allegorical prologue do you prefer? Bit derivative, don't you think? Ovid's mark all over it.').

If all else fails, mention Thomas Tyrwhitt (1730-1786) who established the Chaucer canon. Nobody will know what you mean, but they'll all nod wisely.

It's worth remembering, too, that Chaucer created a number of phrases that have passed into general usage:

'Mordre wil out', 'the smyler with the knyf under the cloke', 'trouthe is the hyeste thing that man may kepe', 'as lene was his hors as is a rake', 'he was a verray parfit gentil knight', 'the lyf so short, the craft so longe to lerne', 'right as an aspen leef she gan to quake', 'entente is al, and nought the lettres'. The trouble is, he couldn't spell.

EDMUND SPENSER (1552-1599)

Poets were so discouraged by the success of Chaucer that it took 200 years for the next one to make a name of any sort and even he spent his whole life doing things reluctantly. Spenser reluctantly went to live and work in Ireland, where he wrote much of his best-known poem, *The Faerie Queene*. Some consider him to be as great a poet as Chaucer, and certainly his spelling was a lot better. Unfortunately, several books of *The Faerie Queene* were burnt when Spenser's castle at Kilcolman was set on fire by the locals in 1598. Spenser reluctantly returned to London, where he became reluctantly very poor and very soon died. Apparently reluctantly.

Like most sixteenth-century poets, Spenser oozed admiration for Elizabeth I, and *The Faerie Queene* would have been an interminable tribute to her if the good people of Kilcolman hadn't had the sense to burn such a lot of it. It fills six books – Spenser intended 18. Like any poem of such length, it is monotonous, though Spenser did invent a new form of stanza, in which a ninth line of 12 syllables is added to eight lines of 10 syllables, with a rhyming scheme of abab/bcbc/c.

You may well already know a line of Spenser:

Sweet Thames run softly, till I end my song

This comes from the poem *Prothalamion*. Everyone else will think it is some kind of drug, so you can chatter at length about it being written (reluctantly) in 1596 to celebrate the double marriage of Lady Elizabeth and Lady Katherine Somerset (not to each other, to be clear).

NUMEROUS KNIGHTS

The sixteenth century also saw a vast number of knights and nobles writing verse in between voyaging round the world, dying heroically in foreign fields and having their heads cut off, though their poetry was seldom that bad. The best known are Sir Thomas Wyatt, Sir Walter Raleigh, Sir Philip Sidney, Henry Howard, Earl of Surrey, and Fulke Greville, Lord Brooke.

SIR THOMAS WYATT (1503-1542)

Wyatt was one of Anne Boleyn's lovers (allegedly), but timed his (alleged) affair wisely, i.e., before her marriage to Henry VIII.

You may already know some lines of Wyatt:

They flee from me who sometime did me seek

Noli me tangere ; for Cæsar's I am,

And wild for to hold, though I seem tame.

And wilt thou leave me thus?

The last of these he thought so good that he used it several times.

SIR WALTER RALEIGH (1552-1618)

Few know that Sir Walter really spelt his name Ralegh. It's advisable to abide by this, as by his time even poets' spelling had improved beyond all recognition, though they still had trouble with 'desyre', 'promysse', 'despayre', and went completely to pieces with 'ioye' (eye). The night before he died, Ralegh wrote a clever and moving poem, 'The Lie', referring to his execution with a wit and frankness that can't have been easy. It's worth reading.

SIR PHILIP SIDNEY (1554-1586)

Sir Philip Sidney was one of a group who formed the Areopagus Club for the purpose of naturalising the classic metres in English verse. Those who turned up to the inaugural meeting brandishing spears of a certain green vegetable from their allotments were disappointed to find no mention of vegetables. Sidney is remembered for two things: passing up a drink as he was dying on the battlefield of Zutphen ('Thy necessity is yet greater than mine') and writing several famous poems, most starting with the letter A ('Arcadia', 'Apologie for Poetrie', 'Astrophel', atcetera).

He also wrote a prose work about poetry – *The Defence of Poesy* – in which he attacked some of the lesser bards of his time: 'There have been many most excellent poets that never versified, and now swarm many versifiers that need never answer to the name of poets.'

SUBLIME SHAKESPEARE (1564-1616)

There are two vital pieces of information about Shakespeare. First, that he wanted to be remembered as a poet only. Second, that he didn't write a great deal of poetry: *The Rape of Lucrece, Venus and Adonis,* 'The Phoenix and the Turtle' and more than 150 sonnets.

The Rape of Lucrece is a poem of seven-lined stanzas on the subject of Lucretia, whose beauty inflames Sextus Tarquinius, son of the King of Rome, to such an extent (so he says) that he can't control himself. Lucretia commits suicide, and the entire Tarquinius family is booted out of Rome and replaced by a republican government. *Venus and Adonis* is a poem of six-lined stanzas, probably Shakespeare's first published work, about the inability of Venus to dissuade the youthful Adonis from going hunting and getting himself killed by a wild boar – serves him right. 'The Phoenix and the Turtle' is a mocking, tragic poem – possibly about a mock turtle and a mock phoenix – both of whom perish in their love. Be warned: very few of Shakespeare's poems, or anybody else's for that matter, have happy endings.

But it is the *Sonnets* that are his finest verse works. Published in 1609, and probably written between 1593 and 1596, they fall into several groups. Nobody is quite sure who they are dedicated to, mainly on account of the enigmatic dedication that precedes the poems: 'TO.THE. ONLIE.BEGETTER.OF.THESE.INSUING.SONNETS, Mr.W.H.ALL.HAPPINESSE.' Main candidates include the Earl of Pembroke (William Herbert) and the Earl of Southampton

(Henry Wriothesley – yes, this would mean that the initials are reversed, but since when have such details stopped a good theory?). Assume an air of studied indifference whenever some proselytising poetry buff attempts to convert you to his pet theory about this age-old question. Not so much a whodunnit as a who'dhedunnitwith, this 'mystery' about the identity of the dedicatee of the sonnets is a bore's paradise, and the less you engage with it the better for your mental health and general well-being. Some familiarity with the sonnets themselves is recommended, however, as this sonnet sequence forms one of the highest points of the canon. You don't have to read the things, of course; suffice to know that they are, broadly speaking, addressed to three people – the fair youth, a rival poet and a dark lady.

There are many well-known quotations from the *Sonnets*; here are a few that you might want to be able to trot out:

Shall I compare thee to a summer's day? (18)

Lilies that fester smell far worse than weeds. (94)

My mistress' eyes are nothing like the sun. (130)

Love is not love which alters when it alteration finds. (116)

The expense of spirit in a waste of shame
Is lust in action. (129)

Bare ruin'd choirs, where late the sweet birds sang. (73)

Over and above that, pick a number, any number, learn a few lines other than the first, and look knowledgeable.

'Gothic revival' is an exciting phrase, perhaps a desperate attempt to make eighteenth-century poetry sound interesting. It isn't.

THE METAPHYSICALS TO THE ROMANTICS, AND MORE

THE METAPHYSICALS

Why were they called the 'Metaphysical Poets'? Why not. You see, that's the sort of air of mystery they cultivated. If you find yourself having to define the term, fall back on the following words: figurative, visionary, incorporeal. Then change the subject.

JOHN DONNE (1572-1631)

John Donne, ex-Roman Catholic, secret marrier, part-time soldier, Anglican cleric and great preacher, was the greatest of the metaphysical poets, writing verse in which passion and reason are disappointingly interwoven. This is exemplified in one line from his poem 'The Cannonization':

For God's sake hold your tongue, and let me love.

But, of course, Donne couldn't hold his tongue. No poet has ever been able to do this. Still, if you can forgive the tricksy cleverness, then Donne's work can be rather:

1. Energetic:

Batter my heart, three-personed God.
(Holy Sonnets)

Busy old fool, unruly Sun,
Why dost thou thus,
Through windows, and through curtains, call on us?
('The Sun Rising')

2. Erotic:

Licence my roving hands, and let them go
Before, behind, between, above, below.
O, my America, my new-found-land.
(Elegy XX: 'To His Mistress Going To Bed')

3. Entomologic:

Mark but this flea, and mark in this,
How little that which thou deniest me is;
It suck'd me first, and now sucks thee,
And in this flea our two bloods mingled be.
('The Flea')

JOHN MILTON (1608–1674)

John Milton's poetry is excellent if you don't try to read more than 12 lines without a break of at least three weeks.

Having served in Cromwell's government, Milton was arrested at the Restoration and heavily fined. Shortly afterwards, understandably, he wrote *Paradise Lost*. Things picked up financially and he wrote *Paradise Regained*.

Nobody knows why he wrote *Samson Agonistes*, so you can have a field day here. Be careful, however, about drawing any easy analogies between Samson's blindness and Milton's own (he was blind by the age of 44). Nothing, absolutely nothing, is easy in Milton. Nor, for that matter, are there any jokes. At all. And dying of gout – something few poets had achieved since the Roman Ennius – can't have been much of a laugh either.

If you must read some Milton, steer clear of the 10,000-line *Paradise Lost* and head for the shorter stuff. Allow your eyes to moisten soulfully as you recite some of the most poignant lines in English literature from sonnets such as 'On his blindness' ('They also serve who only stand and wait') and 'On his late deceased wife' ('Methought I saw my late espoused saint / Brought to me like Alcestis from the grave'). Alternatively, adopt an air of supreme nonchalance and say, 'When it comes to Milton, I'm with Pound', the American modernist poet who wrote him off for his 'asinine bigotry' and 'the coarseness of his mentality'. Some might suggest that Pound was referring to himself.

THE RESTORATION POETS

The Restoration period was best known for its impatience with the lyrical excesses of the Metaphysicals. 'Clarity' was the key word. The names to look out for are Herrick, Waller (Edmund, not Fats), Butler, Marvell, Dryden and Anon. But the actual school boundaries are blurred; many academicians, for example, believe that Marvell was a

Metaphysical (or are they confusing him with a magician on Great Yarmouth pier?).

ROBERT HERRICK (1591-1674)

Robert Herrick's poetry appears to be heavily influenced by the horticultural,

Fair daffodils, we weep to see...

I sing of brooks, of blossoms, birds and bowers...

Cherry ripe, ripe, ripe, I cry...

but is really extremely sensuous. Even one of his most famous 'flowery' lines,

Gather ye rosebuds while ye may,

is the opening of a poem entitled 'To the Virgins, to Make Much of Time' and his other titles include 'No Difference i' th' Dark' and 'Delight in Disorder' ('A sweet disorder in the dress / kindles in clothes a wantonness'). Other poems of Herrick's – 'Her Legs' ('Fain would I kiss my Julia's dainty leg'); 'Upon Julia's Breasts' ('Between whose glories, there my lips I'll lay') – might single Herrick out as the Benny Hill of English letters. Were someone to suggest to you such a travesty of critical opinion, you should adopt a tone of gravitas, or what passes for it, as you explain that Herrick was no smutty adolescent but rather, simply, that rarest of rare things, the über-oxymoron: the contented poet.

EDMUND WALLER (1606-1687)

Edmund Waller managed to avoid being executed by the Roundheads by betraying all his Royalist associates (probably in heroic couplets) and spent the rest of his life writing poems of polished simplicity and fawning gratitude to whomever was in power, e.g., 'Panegyric to My Lord Protector', 'His Majesty's Escape At St Andere'. On the side, he wrote several poems in praise of various women.

SAMUEL BUTLER (1612-1680)

Samuel Butler has the distinction of being the first poet to make a reference to 'punk':

> And made them fight, like mad or drunk
> For Dame Religion as for punk...

This comes from his best-known poem, *Hudibras*, for which he was given a lump sum of £300 and a pension of £100 a year by Charles II, making it very hard for Butler to die in penury, but, like most poets, he managed to do so.

ANDREW MARVELL (1621-1678)

Like Louise Mensch, Andrew Marvell was first a poet and later an MP – but you would be advised to try this progression the other way round. In the former capacity he wrote many poems in praise of gardens and country life, thus beginning a trend which has unhappily flourished among versifiers ever since. His best-known work is comfortably 'To His Coy Mistress', probably the most celebrated example of the *carpe diem* (or 'let's get on with it') poem, a form – strangely

– more favoured by men-versifiers than women. Quite the most wonderful piece of male bluffery ('Had we but world enough, and time, / This coyness, Lady, were no crime.'), it is a great pity that history does not relate whether the poem actually did the trick or not.

Marvell's second most famous poem may be his 'Horatian Ode upon Cromwell's Return from Ireland', which goes so far in eulogising the warty General that it's hard to believe it isn't sarcastic:

[The Irish] can affirm his praises best,
And have, though overcome, confest
How good he is, how just,
And fit for highest trust.

Such sycophancy could only lead to a career in politics. Marvell became MP for Hull.

JOHN DRYDEN (1631-1700)

John Dryden was the first official Poet Laureate, though not all his poetry is bad. He wrote an enormous number of poems, many of them unreadably long, but you could try dipping into 'Absalom and Achitophel' (only a few thousand lines long) or 'Alexander's Feast' (sometimes known as the 'Second Song for St Cecilia's Day'), which contains perhaps his best-known line: 'None but the brave deserves the fair'; or 'MacFlecknoe', a satirical work that attacks one of Dryden's contemporaries, a poet with the less-than-lyrical name Shadwell. In Dryden's poem, Shadwell's pre-eminence in the realm of dullness leads him to being crowned at the Barbican, which shows remarkable foresight on the part of Dryden. He was clearly a man not without wit, but translating the entire works of Virgil must do something to you.

ANON

The best poems of the early period, however, were written by the famous Anon, and include 'Sir Patrick Spens' (namechecked in Coleridge's 'Dejection: An Ode'), 'Greensleeves' (one of Henry VIII's favourite poems), and ballads such as 'Robin Hood and Allan-a-Dale'. A ballad is a simple poem, usually spirited, invariably understandable, written in short stanzas and narrating a popular story. Bluffers should point out the shame that we seldom know who wrote poems that are understandable, but we always know who wrote the incomprehensible, and suggest that it probably has something to do with the Meaning of Life.

GOTHIC REVIVAL

This term refers to a part of the eighteenth century when many writers became obsessed with the frightening and supernatural. It's an exciting phrase, perhaps a desperate attempt to make eighteenth-century poetry sound interesting. It isn't.

All the poets of the eighteenth century are incredibly dull: Pope, Thomson, Johnson, Gray, Goldsmith, Cowper and a host of others. Don't bother with any of them. They spent half their time writing dull verse, and the other half criticising the dullness of others. Alexander Pope even wrote an interminable poem on the subject, *The Dunciad*, a mock-paean to the goddess of Dulness (correctly spelt), daughter of Nox and Chaos; quite quotable ('A brain of feathers, and a heart of lead') but maybe a tad knowing and something of a soft target.

ALEXANDER POPE (1688-1744)

Arguably, Pope was the least dull and could be said to have cornered the market in satirical poems of the period. If nothing else, he bequeathed the English language two of its most enduring clichés:

Damn with faint praise...

and

Who breaks a butterfly upon a wheel?

JAMES THOMSON (1700-1748)

James Thomson moved a little away from the artificiality of most of them, but is to be forever condemned for writing 'Rule, Britannia!'

SAMUEL JOHNSON (1709-1784)

Johnson's poems are as leadenly witty as was his conversation.

THOMAS GRAY (1716-1771)

Thomas Gray wrote 'Elegy Written in a Country Churchyard'. Any bluffer worth his salt should memorise the opening to this famous and influential poem (which, incidentally, provides the source of the phrase *Far From*

The Madding Crowd which Thomas Hardy was to adopt for his novel over a century later):

> *The curfew tolls the knell of parting day,*
> *The lowing herd wind slowly o'er the lea,*
> *The plowman homeward plods his weary way,*
> *And leaves the world to darkness and to me.*

Great stuff. Transcendental and inspired though poets may be on occasion, they are also inveterately incontinent and rarely know when to shut up. Gray, for example, was also responsible for the following, the opening of which is quoted in full – not for you to memorise, but merely to demonstrate that while we all have our off days, at least ours are not preserved for all eternity to snigger at:

> *Twas on a lofty vase's side,*
> *Where China's gayest art had dyed*
> *The azure flowers that blow,*
> *Demurest of the tabby kind,*
> *The pensive Selima, reclined,*
> *Gazed on the lake below.*
> ('On The Death Of A Favourite Cat,
> Drowned In A Tub Of Gold Fishes').

OLIVER GOLDSMITH (1730-1774)

Oliver Goldsmith wrote one poem ('The Deserted Village') from which most are familiar with:

> *And fools, who came to scoff, remained to pray.*

WILLIAM COWPER (1731-1800)

William Cowper was bullied at school, tried to commit suicide and wrote 'The Diverting History of John Gilpin' to divert himself from melancholia. He didn't succeed.

WORTHY MENTIONS

With the exception of Chatterton (*see* 'Poets and Death'), none of the eighteenth-century poets managed to die in an interesting way, and we've already told you how dull most of them are. Despite this, you could commend five poems from this period:

1. 'Tom Bowling' by Charles Dibdin

Not only a rattling good poem, but a most moving song. George II was so moved that he reportedly granted Dibdin a lump sum of £1,000 and a pension of several hundred pounds a year, simply for writing this one work.

2. 'The Tyger' by William Blake

Dreadfully spelt but wonderfully written.

3. 'Jerusalem', also by Blake

Moves even atheists and English rugby fans.

4. 'Tam o'Shanter' by Robert Burns

Impossible to understand unless you speak old Scots, but none the less enjoyable for a' that.

5. 'A Red, Red Rose', also by Burns

With the possible exception of Dibdin, these poets are well known and many will write off their work as mere songs or popularist, lightweight stuff. What the bluffer needs to do, therefore, is approach the poems in a solemn and heavyweight fashion. Point out, for example, that in 'Jerusalem', we have a clear exposition of Blake's Theory of Imagination, 'the real and eternal world of which the Vegetable Universe is but a faint shadow.' People will start thinking of artichokes and won't understand, which is the secret to talking about poetry.

In the case of Burns, make much of the conflict within him: sympathy with the ardour of the French revolutionaries on the one hand, but a propensity to convivial living on the other. Suggest how different things would have been had he taken passage to Jamaica as he planned at the age of 27. He could have been the first Scottish reggae poet and rapper. If all else fails, just recite the odd line of Burns – you'll be amazed:

a) how much of it you know already
b) how quickly the room is cleared.

As your trump card, have ready the information that Blake never and Burns rarely went to school.

THE ROMANTICS

The Romantics managed to lead appropriately romantic lives. Leigh Hunt was imprisoned for writing a critical article on the Prince Regent in 1813, and also introduced Keats and Shelley. The Irish poet Thomas Moore (no one will have heard of him, so 'I have always thought the work of Moore rather unfairly eclipsed by his contemporaries' is pretty much a risk-free bluff) accumulated debts of £6,000 in Bermuda and managed to pay them off. Walter Scott ran up debts of £114,000 and worked himself to death in an attempt to pay his creditors. Southey was expelled from Westminster School for a precocious essay against flogging, spent a life stuffed with domestic misfortunes, and died, as we have heard, of softening of the brain. Charles Wolfe died romantically young, at the age of 32, and some have unkindly called his most famous poem, 'The Burial of Sir John Moore', a 'mere freak of intellect'. Byron liked the poem but reckoned that someone else, probably Thomas Campbell, wrote it, and there has been dispute over the authorship ever since.

THE GIANTS OF POETRY
(OR THE SCHOOL OF ILL HEALTH)

Apart from the Lake Poets (*see* page 59), the Giants of English Poetry are Byron, Shelley and Keats, who between them managed only 90 years of life. When you consider that Tennyson lived to be 83 all on his own, you can appreciate the full truth of Daniel Defoe's couplet:

The best of men cannot suspend their fate
The good die early, and the bad die late
('The Character of the late Dr S Annesley')

GEORGE GORDON, LORD BYRON (1788-1824)

Most of Byron's poetry is described by experts as 'Byronic', which shows how easy it is to be an expert on poetry.

Byronic means rebelling against the conventional morality, defying fate, and being contemptuous of the society that Byron scorned and left. But Byron's poetry was also proud, moody, cynical, defiant, full of revenge, often deeply moving and beautiful. Byron's great gift was his ability to write immensely long poems which are also totally readable, but you could go for something short like 'She Walks in Beauty' – only 18 lines and every one a winner – or the rollicking 'The Destruction of Sennacherib':

> *The Assyrian came down like the wolf on the fold,*
> *And his cohorts were gleaming in purple and gold.*

This one is a classic example of the use of the anapest (*see* 'Glossary'). Make sure you know what this term means if this poem is going to make an appearance in any of your bluffs.

PERCY BYSSHE SHELLEY (1792-1822)

Shelley, too, led a romantic life. He was sent down from Oxford in 1811 for writing a pamphlet entitled 'The Necessity of Atheism'. He married at the age of 18 and again (to Mary of *Frankenstein* fame) at 24, after his first wife drowned herself in the Serpentine. His poetry is ferocious and beautiful, and he used it to great effect in his attacks on Castlereagh's Tory administration ('The Mask of Anarchy') and George IV's matrimonial affairs (*Oedipus Tyrannus; or Swellfoot the Tyrant*). It seems a shame that he's remembered, via English Literature syllabi, chiefly for his softer, admittedly graceful, poetry such as 'Ode to the West

Wind', 'To a Skylark' and 'Ozymandias' (pronounced with the stress on 'mand' and not on 'i' of 'ias'; a small point, perhaps, but a faux pas many a bluffer has committed).

JOHN KEATS (1795-1821)

The wonder is that Keats wrote any poetry at all in his short life, ravaged by consumption and nursing his brother, Tom, whom he loved and who predeceased him by three years. But Keats wrote several long poems ('Endymion', 'Hyperion' and 'Lamia' – all of them subsequently given as names to famous racehorses), some of the finest odes in the English language ('To a Nightingale', 'To Autumn', 'On a Grecian Urn'), and some 40 sonnets ('On First Looking into Chapman's Homer', 'On the Grasshopper and Cricket' and 'To Sleep').

Be unstinting in your praise of Keats, who received only bad reviews in his short lifetime (at the hands of the Tory press because he was a friend of Leigh Hunt), and who has received only glowing tributes since his death. Samuel Taylor Coleridge and Keats met only once, in 1819, and then only very briefly. 'There is death in that hand', Coleridge recorded himself as having said to his walking companion as he turned away after shaking the young man's mitt. An impressive example of Coleridge's medical intuition and gift for empathy? Or simply a tremendous bluff on STC's part (the passage ends with 'yet this was, I believe, before the consumption showed itself distinctly' so was clearly written with the benefit of hindsight)? You decide.

THE LAKES, THE PATRIOTS AND THE WAR POETS

THE LAKE POETS

The most famous poets who lived in England's Lake District around the turn of the nineteenth century are William Wordsworth and Samuel Taylor Coleridge, who met in their early twenties, formed an intense friendship, fell out badly and made up a couple of years later (though it was never quite the same again).

WILLIAM WORDSWORTH (1770-1850)

Wordsworth was an early supporter of the French Revolution (indeed, he pinned his political colours to the mast by impregnating a French girl called Annette Vallon on a cross-Channel trip), wrote some wonderful poems – 'Lines Composed a Few Miles Above Tintern Abbey', 'Composed Upon Westminster Bridge', 'The Solitary Reaper' and (with Coleridge) *Lyrical Ballads* – and then went all small-c-conservative and ended up as Poet Laureate. While it would be difficult, nay a little stupid, to argue that Wordsworth is anything but one of the major English poets, should anyone deny that the quality of Wordsworth's poetry trailed off significantly in later years, you can state with absolute certainty that they are talking out of their hat. Or postman's cap. In 1813 Wordsworth accepted the post of Distributor of Stamps for Westmorland (to the tune of £400 per annum) – hardly the stuff of radicals (and indeed young guns Shelley, Byron and Keats all accused Wordsworth of apostasy) – and was unable to recapture the freshness and newness of his earlier work.

SAMUEL TAYLOR COLERIDGE (1772-1834)

Coleridge led a more interesting life, albeit with the help of opium, but wrote less revered poetry than Wordsworth. Nowadays, people only tend to remember 'The Rime of the Ancient Mariner' (the longest poem in *Lyrical Ballads,* the radical collection of poetry which he and Wordsworth jointly contributed to) and 'Kubla Khan'. As young men, Coleridge and Southey devoted themselves to Pantisocracy, which sounds dirty but was in fact a form of communism which they intended to practise on the banks of the Susquehanna River in Pennsylvania, where, presumably, no one would see them. The project never got off the ground.

Of Coleridge's less-well-known works, you may want to familiarise yourself with 'Christabel', a two-part Gothic fantasy spanning the worlds of psychopathology and the supernatural. There was to be a third part but Coleridge never wrote it; he also did not finish 'The Wanderings of Cain' and his excuse for 'Kubla Khan' being a mere fragment of what would have been a longer poem was that his recollection of the (opium-fuelled) dream, which the poem was to be an account of, was disturbed by a 'person on business from Porlock'. Have no truck with any of this bluff and bluster; most poets are slackers who overindulge in the drugs of choice of their particular age.

Poetry buffs are very fond of backing their man in the eternal Wordsworth v Coleridge debate. You can afford to assume a distant look of ennui if you ever have the misfortune to be caught up in this particular stalemate. If you can be bothered to take part in the discussion, you might consider suggesting a compromise option: that both men were geniuses but in very different ways. Such even-handedness is beyond all so-called experts and academics and, after dropping this seemingly innocuous but bomb-like assertion, you should withdraw at your earliest convenience.

JINGO LINGO

The nineteenth century is crammed with poets fighting to declaim their patriotic fervour: Macaulay, Tennyson, Newbolt, Austin, Kipling and scores of other lesser-known and even worse poets.

THOMAS BABINGTON MACAULAY (1800-1859)

Another MP and poet, Macaulay's poems are all about heroes and heroines, and battles, some of them amazingly awful:

They are here! They rush on! We are broken! We are gone!

Our left is borne before them like stubble on the blast.

O Lord, put forth thy might! O Lord, defend the right!

Stand back to back in God's name, and fight it to the last.

Maybe he was a good MP.

ALFRED, LORD TENNYSON (1809-1892)

Not all of Tennyson's poetry is awful, which is surprising when you realise that:

a) he became Poet Laureate
b) he was given a pension of £200 by Sir Robert Peel
c) Queen Victoria thought he was wonderful.

Try to forget 'The Revenge', 'The May Queen' and 'The Defence of Lucknow', and concentrate on 'Crossing the Bar', 'Locksley Hall' ('In the spring a young man's fancy lightly turns to thoughts of love'), 'Morte d'Arthur' and the incomparable 'In Memoriam'. Some lines from this 133-stanza poem, which was written in response to the sudden death of his closest friend, Arthur Hallam, have passed into the fabric of the language (for example, 'Nature, red in tooth and claw'; ''Tis better to have loved and lost / Than never to have loved at all').

Tennyson is equally famous for a short poem which memorialises the bravery of the British cavalry in their defeat at the hands of the Russians. Led into battle by a Lieutenant called Lord Cardigan at a Ukrainian town called Balaclava, 'The Charge of the Light Brigade' is by some distance the most moving and impressive poem ever to be inspired by knitwear in the entire poetic canon.

SIR HENRY NEWBOLT (1862-1938)

So bad, he's essential. Newbolt should have been Poet Laureate, and may well have spent his entire adult life believing that he was. Read all his poems, learn them by heart; they will take away the very breath of any expert or critic. Take 'Clifton Chapel':

To set the cause above renown,
To love the game beyond the prize,
To honour, while you strike him down,
The foe that comes with fearless eyes.

Many of Newbolt's poems have been set to music ('Drake's Drum', 'The Old Superb') which makes them even better. You can sing them at the critics and intellectuals.

Robert Bridges thought 'Drake's Drum' wonderful – 'I wish I had ever written anything half as good' – which tells you all you need to know about Robert Bridges. Newbolt's poetry was amazingly popular. *Admirals All* is said to have run to four editions in a fortnight in 1897.

ALFRED AUSTIN (1835-1913)

Austin was by and large an unsuccessful poet with an understandably wavering faith in his poetic genius. He was a man of forthright political views – he rejoiced in Prussia's military dominance in 1870, thought Garibaldi 'an unmitigated nuisance', and wrote a most unfortunate ode celebrating the Boer War's Jameson Raid. Austin worked on the principle that no poem could be great unless it was an epic on a theme combining love, patriotism and religion (you'd be amazed how many poems do).

RUDYARD KIPLING (1865-1936)

Many people are astonished to learn that Kipling won the Nobel Prize in Literature in 1907, but then they probably haven't read the Polish novels of Henryk Sienkiewicz who won the prize in 1905, or the Italian poems of Giosuè Carducci, who won in 1906. The point is that it's not essential to write off Kipling's poetry simply because it scans and rhymes. Point out that his work is all quotations:

For the female of the species is more deadly than the male

What stands if Freedom fall?

Who dies if England live?

It's clever, but is it Art?

To the legion of the lost ones,
To the cohort of the damned

You're a better man than I am, Gunga Din!

…the flannelled fools at the wicket or the muddied oafs at the goals

On the road to Mandalay

The Captains and the Kings depart

Brandy for the Parson

Sussex by the Sea

Take up the White Man's burden…

The whole of the poem *If.*

The trouble with Kipling is that he lived a reasonably long time and died from natural causes, which precludes him from being a great poet.

OTHER NINETEENTH-CENTURY GENIUSES

Apart from the Brownings and the Rossettis, who came in couplets, most other nineteenth-century poets were part-timers. Novelist poets included William Makepeace Thackeray, Emily Brontë, Charles Kingsley, Matthew Arnold, George Meredith, Thomas Hardy and Robert Louis Stevenson. William Morris wrote poetry when he wasn't wallpapering. Lewis Carroll wrote poetry when he wasn't doing sums or taking photographs of young girls. Edward Lear invented the limerick. Oscar Wilde wrote poetry when he wasn't being delightfully outrageous with a hock and seltzer.

ROBERT BROWNING (1812-1889) AND ELIZABETH BARRETT BROWNING (1806-1861)

Probably the most famous thing the Brownings did was to elope, but Robert Browning also wrote *The Pied Piper of Hamelin.* Most people know the story of the first two-thirds of the poem but forget that, at the end, the children emerge in Transylvania. There is a great deal of wit in the poems of Robert Browning and a great deal of beauty in the poems of Elizabeth Barrett Browning, especially in her *Sonnets from the Portuguese.* Unlike most poets, the Brownings lived more excitingly than they died.

DANTE GABRIEL ROSSETTI (1828-1882) AND CHRISTINA ROSSETTI (1830-1894)

Dante Gabriel Rossetti was a painter and poet who, along with William Holman Hunt and John Everett Millais, founded the pre-Raphaelite Brotherhood. Dante Rossetti's poetry is now overshadowed by his sister Christina's, which has been compared to Emily Dickinson. This means that it is a) short, b) desperate and c) tremendous.

The award for the most miserable English poet is fiercely contested. Hardy could probably be a contender; Larkin worth a punt; Hopkins must surely be in with a shout. But you would be on safe ground if you were to put in a word for Christina Rossetti for this particular contribution:

I looked for that which is not, nor can be,
And hope deferred made my heart sick in truth
But years must pass before a hope of youth
Is resigned utterly.

GERARD MANLEY HOPKINS (1844-1889)

If not quite the most miserable, you could suggest that the most interesting poet of his time was Gerard Manley Hopkins who wrote such bizarre and original poetry that none of it was published until 30 years after his death, which is a sure-fire but rather disappointing way of becoming a cult figure. Having forsworn the writing of poetry upon becoming a Jesuit priest, he was moved to come out of retirement at the age of 31 by reading of the death of five nuns in a shipwreck. There is no need whatsoever to read the poem itself, the highly baroque and largely incomprehensible 'The Wreck of the Deutschland'. Hopkins is best known for his technique ('sprung rhythm') which relates to his sensual poems, not to his sensual life. Refer to 'inscape' (the essence of an object) and 'instress' (what happens when inscape is understood by the reader). Hopkins's *Terrible Sonnets* ('I wake and feel the fell of dark, not day') are really very good; written in the last years of his life, their titular adjective refers to their horrifying quality rather than suggesting their inadequacy.

THOMAS HARDY (1840-1928)

Although much better known in his lifetime as a novelist than a poet, Thomas Hardy thought of himself primarily as a poet, the novels being a means to earn a living more than anything. His poetry – whose range is vast in terms of both subject matter and form – is still somewhat overshadowed by his novels, however. Shot through with a wry pessimism, as some of the titles of his poetry collections attest – *Satires of Circumstance,* for example, and *Time's Laughingstocks and Other Verses* – Hardy's poetry has a rugged honesty which was to become a beacon of clarity for later poets such as Philip Larkin. Famous poems include 'In Time of "The Breaking of Nations"' and 'The Convergence of the Twain'; somewhat less familiar and safer territory for the bluffer are *Poems of*

1912-1913, the immensely moving sequence of poems, and exploration of grief, which Hardy wrote after the sudden death of his wife, Emma. This sequence is perhaps made all the more remarkable, and poignant, by the fact that he and his wife – despite continuing to share the same house – had hardly spoken for years prior to her death.

Anyway, whatever his relationship with his wife, a mere year after her death, old Hardy was sticking his trumpet major elsewhere: he married his nubile young 'friend', Florence Dugdale, who was almost 40 years younger than he. Poets. Tut.

THE WAR POETS: FIRST WORLD WAR

Rupert Brooke, TP Cameron Wilson, Leslie Coulson, Jeffery Day, Julian Grenfell, WN Hodgson, TE Hulme, Thomas Kettle, Francis Ledwidge, EA Mackintosh, RB Marriott-Watson, John McCrae, Wilfred Owen, Nowell Oxland, Robert Palmer, Isaac Rosenberg, Alan Seeger, Patrick Shaw-Stewart, Charles Sorley, EW Tennant and Edward Thomas are just some of the poets who fought and died in the First World War. They were all young, egocentric, talented and almost forced into verse by the horror of their experiences. Some critics have suggested that it was the static nature of their nightmare existence, creating a fruitful routine, that accounts for the excellence of the poetry of this time; fewer poems written in the Second World War are reckoned in the same class.

Edmund Blunden, himself a soldier in the war, thought that the term 'war poet' was inaccurately applied to many of his contemporaries. Some (Brooke, Siegfried Sassoon, Thomas, Robert Graves, David Jones) were poets who happened to be caught in Armageddon but whose work encompassed many other themes. Others, like Wilfred Owen, had time to write only of war.

WILFRED OWEN (1893-1918)

Owen wrote in the preface to his posthumously published collected poems: 'My subject is War, and the pity of War. The poetry is in the pity.' Had he lived, however (he was killed a week before Armistice Day at the age of 25), who knows what other poetic feats he may have gone on to? Some might argue that Owen's death is the single biggest catastrophe to befall poetry since the death of Keats; others may demur and cite the flowery affectation of his pre-war poetry to illustrate why Owen may not have been able to reach the heights of his war poetry in times of peace.

Futility

Move him into the sun –
Gently its touch awoke him once,
At home, whispering of fields unsown.
Always it awoke him, even in France,
Until this morning and this snow.
If anything might rouse him now
The kind old sun will know.

Think how it wakes the seeds –
Woke, once, the clays of a cold star.
Are limbs so dear-achieved, are sides

Full-nerved – still warm –too hard to stir?
Was it for this the clay grew tall?
– O what made fatuous sunbeams toil
To break earth's sleep at all?

There is little one can really say about this small but perfectly formed poem. Not that artistic achievement borne of great suffering has ever prevented your average poetry buff from sounding off about the merits of this or that aspect of form or metre, or whatever; and in the case of this poem there's always the chance that the reverent silence, which is really the only appropriate response to it, will be broken by someone wittering on about Owen's mastery of pararhyme (a kind of rhyme where the consonant remains the same but the vowel changes – e.g., seeds/sides; tall/toil). 'My great-grandfather was killed at Ypres, you know' is always a pretty effective way of shutting up someone who won't let the poetry of war speak for itself.

SECOND WORLD WAR

Because of the success and fame of the war poets of 1914-1918, a cry went up at the beginning of the 1939-1945 War: 'Where are the war poets?'. Cyril Connolly's sharp retort was, 'Under your nose', and the dreadful days of death once again produced some of the best poetry of the century. They also brought about the death of scores more poets: Drummond Allison, Brian Allwood, David Bourne, Clive Branson, Timothy Corsellis, Keith Douglas, James Farrar, Keith Foottit, Stephen Haggard, TR Hodgson,

John Jarmain, David Geraint Jones, Sidney Keyes, Alun Lewis, David Raikes, Richard Spender, Gervase Stewart, Frank Thompson (publicly executed at the age of 23 in Serbia, after fighting with the Bulgarian partisans) and Nigel Weir. Many of them were young pilots in the RAF, and there is an amazingly calm premonition of death in their work. It should also be remembered that a great many other (sometimes better-known) poets were writing during and after the Second World War – John Arlott, Charles Causley, Paul Dehn, Gavin Ewart, Laurie Lee, John Lehmann, Louis MacNeice, Henry Reed, Stephen Spender, Dylan Thomas and Henry Treece (one of The New Apocalyptics) among them.

Few war poets (or any, for that matter – apart from that Keats fellow) have produced work to rival the precocious maturity of Wilfred Owen. However, this poem by Frank Thompson, published a year after his death in 1944, offers a glimpse of what might have been:

An Epitaph For My Friends

As one who, gazing at a vista
Of beauty, sees the clouds close in,
And turns his back in sorrow,
hearing
The thunderclouds begin.
So we, whose life was all before us,
Our hearts with sunlight filled,
Left in the hills our books and
flowers,

Descended, and were killed.
Write on the stone no word of
sadness –
Only the gladness due,
That we, who asked the most
of living,
Knew how to give it too.

Draw your interlocutor's attention to the sublime use of the caesura – a pause mid-line (bluffers should remember this word) after 'Descended' which makes the tumble of 'and were killed', with the landing on the word 'killed', even more bleak somehow.

Of course, some war poets did survive. The following poem by the Australian poet Kenneth Slessor (*see* 'American Poetry and Some of the Rest') is work of sublime depth. It has echoes of Owen in both the language (compare, you may consider bluffing, 'Only the monstrous anger of the guns. / Only the stuttering rifles' rapid rattle' from Owen's 'Anthem for Doomed Youth' and 'the sob and clubbing of the gunfire' in Slessor's poem) and the focus on the pity of warfare.

Beach Burial

Softly and humbly to the Gulf of Arabs
The convoys of dead sailors come;
At night they sway and wander in the waters far under,
But morning rolls them in the foam.

Between the sob and clubbing of the gunfire
Someone, it seems, has time for this,

To pluck them from the shallows and bury them in burrows
And tread the sand upon their nakedness;

And each cross, the driven stake of tidewood,
Bears the last signature of men,
Written with such perplexity, with such bewildered pity,
The words choke as they begin –

'Unknown seaman' – the ghostly pencil
Wavers and fades, the purple drips,
The breath of wet season has washed their inscriptions
As blue as drowned men's lips,

Dead seamen, gone in search of the same landfall,
Whether as enemies they fought,
Or fought with us, or neither; the sand joins them together,
Enlisted on the other front.

It hardly needs repetition but, as a general rule for any discussion of war poetry, feel confident in emphasising that this darkly brilliant and productive period in the history of the genre is proof, if proof were necessary, that great poetry usually comes about as a result of great suffering.

To speak earnestly about the various types of modern poetry, just think of almost any word that ends in -ism (except rheumatism or criticism) and throw it into the conversation as you would beansprouts into a wok.

MODERNISM

Modern poets are those who have decided that the secret of writing verse is not to write verse but to chop up prose and distribute the pieces unfairly

So that
One line may contain a great many syllables,
And another,
One.

In order to stop modern poets sneering at you as they roll their cigarettes or massage their stubble, you should be able to speak earnestly about the various types of modern poetry. It isn't difficult: just think of almost any word that ends in -ism (except rheumatism or criticism) and throw it into the conversation as you would beansprouts into a wok – Symbolism, Imagism, Vorticism, Dadaism, Existentialism, Surrealism, Movementism, New Formalism. It helps, of course, if you have some vague idea as to what these terms mean, and many of them, though not all, do have a meaning.

SYMBOLISM

Founder Baudelaire.

Proponents Mallarmé and Verlaine – not a French department store, but two poets. An enormous number of Russian poets, all of whose first names begin with V: Vladimir Solovyov, Valery Bryusov, Vyacheslav Ivanov, Etceterov.

Period 1880 to 1890s.

Characteristics The symbol is 'the verbal parallel to a pattern of experience' (Kenneth Burke, US critic). The aim of Symbolism is to evoke, rather than describe.

Technique Impressions, intuitions, sensations. All the Symbolists did was to liken life to objects – life is a clockwork toy, a raspberry jelly, a chicken nugget…

CONCRETE POETRY

Founder Apollinaire.

Proponents Too many to list – the best-known British concrete poet is probably Ian Hamilton Finlay.

Period 1900 to present.

Characteristics Emphasis on the physical existence of the poem – what it's written or printed on, the typography used, any artistic embellishments or decorations. Sometimes accompanied by music – this is invariably the worst type.

Technique To build rather than to write a poem. Since

it may be carved in stone or wood, or have metal words welded together, this is a poem you can actually own and stick in your garden.

IMAGISM

Founder Ezra Pound.

Proponents Richard Aldington, 'HD' (Hilda Doolittle – nothing to do with the Doctor), FS Flint (nothing to do with the Captain), Skipwith Cannell, Amy Lowell, William Carlos Williams, Ford Madox Ford (extra points if you refer to him as Ford Madox Hueffer), Allen Upward and John Cournos.

Period 1910 to 1918 (renewed briefly in the late 1920s).

Characteristics Anglo-American. Influenced by the Chinese, Japanese and early Greeks. Purity of diction. Mercifully small poems. Precision of imagery (hence 'Imagism').

Technique 'Direct treatment of "the thing", whether subjective or objective; to use absolutely no word that did not contribute to the presentation; as regarding rhythm – to compose in sequence of the musical phrase, not in sequence of a metronome' (*Poetry* [US magazine] March 1913). It doesn't matter if you don't understand what this means; no one would dare ask you to explain.

VORTICISM

Founder Wyndham Lewis.

Proponent Wyndham Lewis, although the term was

coined by Ezra Pound.

Period 1914-1915 (it didn't really capture the *zeitgeist*).

Characteristic A kind of literary Cubism in which all art was to be related to the machine and modern industrialisation.

Technique Egocentric concern for Wyndham Lewis.

DADAISM

Founder Tristan Tzara.

Proponents Few, though the Sitwells show a little light-hearted influence.

Period 1917 to 1922.

Characteristics The aim of Dada was to be destructive and to deny sense and order, to suppress all logical relationship between ideas by violence and/or a savage, comic irony.

Technique Sit down, write anything you like and eventually an idea or theme will emerge. A godsend, therefore, to all of us without talent. It's a wonder the movement lasted only five years.

EXISTENTIALISM

Founder Kierkegaard, though there have been existential punch-ups between supporters of rival candidates, and those who assert that Existentialism can't have a founder.

Proponents The philosophers and writers Jean-Paul

Sartre, Martin Heidegger, Gabriel Marcel, Albert Camus and Karl Jaspers. Unfortunately for Existentialism (but perhaps fortunately for us) there have been few out-and-out Existentialist poets, although some enthusiasts have tried to claim Samuel Beckett and Charles Bukowski among their number.

Period 1920s to the present.

Characteristics Emphasis on the uniqueness of human experience and essential individuality of life. French flavour, eclectic, full of disgust for the world. Concerned with feelings, most of them unpleasant.

Technique Most existential writing has to include:

a) someone dying, preferably of the meaninglessness of life or from suppurating boils

b) someone being sick

c) someone being bored out of his or her mind

d) someone being hideously poor

e) everyone contemplating suicide.

SURREALISM

Founder Offshoot of the Dadaists.

Proponents (In England) David Gascoyne, Francis Scarfe, Roger Roughton, Philip O'Connor. (In France) André Breton, Paul Éluard, Louis Aragon. Also big in Spain.

Period Mid-1920s to mid-1930s.

Characteristics Hatred of the prevailing system, exploration of the unconscious mind, rational principles, depiction of disembodied male or female genitalia in incongruous settings as if this is a) clever and b) deep.

Technique Automatic writing (as in Dadaism).

MOVEMENTISM
Not strictly a term at all; most people refer to it as The Movement.

Founder Not so much founded, as a term coined in 1954 by JD Scott, literary editor of *The Spectator*, to describe a group of writers who reacted to the (as they saw it) overblown romanticism of poets such as Dylan Thomas.

Proponents Philip Larkin, John Wain, Donald Davie, Robert Conquest, Thom Gunn, Kingsley Amis.

Period 1950s to the mid-1960s, although New Formalism, a movement in the USA in the late twentieth and early twenty-first centuries, which favours a return to metred and rhymed poetry, is highly influenced by it, and by the poetry of Larkin in particular.

Characteristics Tough, ironic, accessible, unsentimental.

Technique Use of precise language and a rejection of the overblown, flowery phrases of Romanticism. The Movement seems finally to have broken the Ancient Greek yoke that had previously bruised the shoulders of English poetry from Chaucer to Rupert Brooke.

NEW FORMALISM
See Movementism.

BLUFFISM
If you've got this far, this needs no further explanation.

The popular image of a poet is
of some skeletal, consumptive figure,
dying of starvation in a garret.
When you read most poets' work,
it's easy to see why this is such
a popular and attractive image.

OTHER SCHOOLS TO KNOW ABOUT

I n addition to a grasp of poetry's origins, development and traditional schools, you should at the very least have a nodding acquaintance with one or more of the following new schools:

THE RUBICUNDS

The popular image of a poet is of a skeletal, consumptive figure, dying of starvation in a garret. When you read most poets' work, it's easy to see why this is such a popular and attractive image. But a select few have combined girth with verse and most of them wrote what may be described as accessible poetry. Tennyson was a large man. John Masefield worked as a deckhand on the old sailing ships.

At the turn of the century a beefy bevy of poets flourished – notably Oscar Wilde, GK Chesterton and Hilaire Belloc. What they lacked in physical dexterity, they made up for in metrical fluency and agility.

OSCAR WILDE (1854-1900)

Oscar Wilde's most famous poem is 'The Ballad of Reading

Gaol'. It's still a powerful blast against capital punishment and it still generates hot tears of passion at the thought of Wilde's imprisonment (for gross indecency with men). All of Wilde's poetry is a delight to read – you could almost believe that he wished to communicate with his readers, which, sadly, would preclude him from being a great poet.

GILBERT KEITH CHESTERTON (1874-1936)

GK Chesterton was very large and red, and was ill-inclined to stand for any nonsense. He called a spondee a spondee. His poetry is shot through with sentiment, religion and a rich thirst. He used his poetry to express his forthright views on almost every subject, and became very popular as a result. It's hugely unfashionable to espouse his poetry today; it would be like whistling a bit of Eric Coates in the queue for a Prom on Boulez Night.

HILAIRE BELLOC (1870-1953)

Hilaire Belloc, a powerfully built man, not only wrote poems which are understandable, he even wrote poems which are funny: *The Bad Child's Book of Beasts, More Beasts (For Worse Children), The Modern Traveller,* and, his best-known, *Cautionary Tales For Children:*

> Now just imagine how it feels
> When first your toes and then your heels,
> And then by gradual degrees,
> Your shins and ankles, calves and knees,
> Are slowly eaten, bit by bit.

THE ONES YOU REALLY NEED TO KNOW

'The Rubaiyat of Omar Khayyam of Naishapur' is one of those many poems that all have heard of, many have read, few can quote and none can recite. The bluffer can steal a march on others with the verse equivalents of the Golden Oldies by referring to 'Famous Short Verses', or quoting from this list of the Good Old Good Ones. Use them now, before everyone else does and while they are wildly out of fashion:

'To Daffodils', Robert Herrick

'Sir Patrick Spens', Anon

'Against Idleness and Mischief
(How doth the little busy bee…)', Isaac Watts

'Loss of the "Royal George"', William Cowper

'The Tyger', William Blake

'To Daffodils', William Wordsworth

'Lochinvar', Sir Walter Scott

'The Lay of the Last Minstrel', Sir Walter Scott

'The Rime of the Ancient Mariner', Samuel Coleridge

'Beth Gelert', William Robert Spencer

'Bishop Hatto', Robert Southey

'The Destruction of Sennacherib', Lord Byron

'Ozymandias', Percy Bysshe Shelley

'No! (November)', Thomas Hood

'Casabianca' (*The boy stood on the burning deck…*),
Felicia Dorothea Hemans

'The May Queen', Alfred, Lord Tennyson

'The Revenge', Alfred, Lord Tennyson

'Break, break, break', Alfred, Lord Tennyson

'The Old Navy' (*The Captain stood on the carronade…*),
Captain Frederick Marryat

'In the Workhouse: Christmas Day'*, George R Sims

'The Shooting of Dan McGrew', Robert W Service

'Vitaï Lampada', Sir Henry Newbolt

'The Listeners', Walter de la Mare

'Sea Fever', John Masefield

THE ENGLISH COWPAT SCHOOL OF VERSE

There runs through English poetry a constant stream of verbal diarrhoea praising all things rural: cornfields, skylarks, meadows, rivers, brooks, cows, duck ponds, mole-catchers, horseflies, sexual deviants, hey-nonny-nons, nosy-parkers, animal carcasses, gin traps, etc. Significantly, such poems have only come into existence in the last couple

---

* Possibly the best poem ever written: a magnificent diatribe about the twin evils of penury and false charity.

of hundred years, i.e., since most of us stopped living in the country. Nowadays, some misguided local authority has only to chop down a diseased tree for someone to write a poem and send it to the papers, and almost every furred or feathered creature or parasite (with the possible exception of the tapeworm) has been the subject of a rapturous ode.

Poets of this school with the best yield are:

JOHN CLARE (1793-1864)

Clare was a herdboy, militiaman, vagrant, farmer and, finally, lunatic. He wrote wonderful poetry full of the buzzing of insects, the heat of noon, rush poles, hazelnuts, ivied oaks and so on.

Clare is regarded by those in the know as something of a special case, and someone for whom they feel great solicitude; be wary of saying anything negative about him (that he couldn't punctuate for toffee, for example). When his name is mentioned, simply look soulful (his was a sad existence, after all – feted by the literary establishment, then largely discarded, spending his last 23 years in Northampton General Lunatic Asylum) and mutter the words, 'Ah, the enclosures, the enclosures'. No one really knows much about the series of Enclosure Acts (which were passed between the middle of the eighteenth and nineteenth centuries and which removed previously existing rights of local people in respect of common land), other than that Clare railed against them in his poems. All that matters is that everyone thinks the whole enclosures business a Very Bad Thing, so no one will question you further on the matter.

EDMUND BLUNDEN (1896-1974)

It has been said that Blunden's greatest service to poetry was his research into and discovery and publication of the hitherto unpublished poems of John Clare. Blunden's own early poems were lavish in their praise of the pastoral, whether 'blotched with mildew', 'black scowling pond', 'cornered weasel', 'sunlit vale' or 'many centuried tree'.

WILLIAM HENRY DAVIES (1871-1940)

Author of *The Autobiography of a Super Tramp*, Davies wrote short poems, full of comedy (he insisted):

> *Where bumble-bees, for hours and hours,*
> *Sit on their soft, fat, velvet bums,*
> *To wriggle out of hollow flowers ...*

A famous freeloader, Davies was associated with the Dymock Poets, a group which included the much better poets Edward Thomas and Robert Frost who made their home near the Gloucestershire village of that name.

Davies's most famous poem, 'Leisure' (a subject dear to many a poet's heart), includes the lines:

> *What is this life if full of care*
> *We have no time to stand and stare*

One of the things about poetry is that it aims to express something universal (on the whole). These lines appear to be an example of this. Having lost a foot while jumping from one freight train to another, he bore his disability with equanimity, spending much of the rest of his life sitting, standing and staring without any apparent urgency.

WALTER DE LA MARE (1873-1956)

It's probably best not to say anything yet about Walter de la Mare. Serves him right for writing about fairies and fancies and things called Tom Noddy. Almost entirely a 'punishment poet'.

ALFRED EDWARD HOUSMAN (1859-1936)

Get extra bluffing points for knowing his first names as he's always called AE. It's still all right to talk about Housman because, although he wrote about cherry blossom, hawthorn, millstreams, nightingales, etc., he also wrote about people being hanged, battles, hard labour and all that.

GEORGIAN POETS

A complete bluff of a name, Georgian Poetry has nothing to do with any George at all, but is the name given to a body of English verse composed from about 1910 to 1930, much of it of a pastoral, rural or rustic nature (*see also* 'The English Cowpat School of Verse'). The poetry itself rapidly became very unfashionable, although a grand bunch of people wrote it: AE Housman, WH Davies, Walter de la Mare, John Masefield, Victoria (Vita) Sackville-West, Robert Graves, Edmund Blunden and others. It was really the last flowering of English verse before it all went modern or whimsical, taking itself either too seriously or not seriously enough.

The surprising thing about the Georgian group is that it

really was a group, with a real leader: Edward Marsh, one-time secretary to Churchill at the Admiralty. The group achieved great popularity for a limited period, but was dealt a swift death blow by Eliot's *The Waste Land*.

AUDEN AND ELIOT

Try to get as little involved as possible with the two literary 'giants' of the twentieth century, WH Auden and TS Eliot. It's always exhausting to take on people who have 'given voice to the disillusionment of their generation', and the race to be the best Auden/Eliot swot began many decades ago, so you're already miles behind. But if you want to compete, here's something to get you out of the starting blocks.

THOMAS STEARNS ELIOT (1888-1965)

Earn points again for knowing these names, as he is always referred to as TS. Open by saying that Eliot suffered all his life from deracination (being torn up by the roots) and aboulia.

Follow this by remarking on his study of Sanskrit and Pali. The only one of Eliot's poems that isn't a dreadful sweat to read is 'The Love Song of J Alfred Prufrock' (his earliest mature poem), and you can wax lyrical about 'the mysterious interstices of this poem, its mixture of colloquialism and elegance, and its memorable ironies', ending by stating that 'the portrait of enervation was executed with contradictory energy'.

Eliot's most famous poem, *The Waste Land,* was written in Margate and Lausanne and published in 1922. It was thought outrageous at the time, but Eliot himself referred to it as 'just a piece of rhythmical grumbling'. It has been hailed as bringing together various kinds of despair – for lost youth, lost love, lost friendship, lost value, lost fountain pen, etc.

Eliot's other major work is the *Four Quartets,* and you get hundreds of points if you know their names: 'Burnt Norton' (1935), 'East Coker' (1940), 'The Dry Salvages' (1941) and 'Little Gidding' (1942).

WH AUDEN (1907-1973)

Double points for knowing that these initials stand for Wystan Hugh – poor chap. Auden cherished the belief that he was of Icelandic origin, which makes you feel that he had a greater claim to deracination than Eliot. When he went to Christ Church, Oxford, he confided in his tutor, Neville Coghill, that his ambition was to be a great poet – you could say that sort of thing in the mid-1920s and get away with it.

He was influenced by Eliot, and decided that poems should be 'verbal artefacts'. He was also influenced by Homer Lane, and took as his theme for poetry 'the healing power of uninhibited love'. Like Eliot he became a teacher (the boys knew him as Uncle Wiz), and then spent the rest of his life making Very Important Decisions. He decided it was wrong to defend freedom against fascism (but though he did go to Spain to volunteer as an ambulance driver for the republicans, he was not accepted for service and eventually came home after only a month).

George Orwell and Auden got into a spat when the

former objected to the latter's use of the phrase 'necessary murder' in his poem *Spain*, arguing that the phrase could only have been written by 'the kind of person who is always somewhere else when the trigger is pulled'. Having had his bluff successfully called, Auden got all sniffy about it for a while, then distanced himself from the poem altogether. After his little holiday in Spain, Auden decided to stay in the USA with his great friend Christopher Isherwood, though unkind people said it was easier to fight fascism (or not) from a distance. In fact, Auden left England for love, having met a young New York poet called Chester Kallman. They wrote the libretto for Stravinsky's *The Rake's Progress* together, but it wasn't always a happy relationship.

Say, loudly and confidently, that Auden wrote no decent poetry after leaving England, save 'The Shield of Achilles' and 'In Praise of Limestone' – he had a thing about rocks.

Auden was obsessively punctual, excessively funny in his youth and liked to mock his religious faith – he often referred to the Almighty as 'Miss God'. In later life he had an overwhelming fear that he would fall down dead in his New York apartment and that his body wouldn't be discovered for over a week. This was probably a ploy to have an interesting death and thus become a truly great poet. In fact, he died in Vienna on 29 September 1973 after a very successful reading of his poems. It seems a little excessive as an encore.

WILLIAM EMPSON (1906-1984)

Perhaps the bluffer's best approach when the conversation turns to Eliot and Auden is to say, 'What about Empson?'

A contemporary of Eliot and Auden, he wrote two volumes of verse, *Poems* and *The Gathering Storm* (a title pinched by Churchill), which are really difficult, full of analytical argument and imagery drawn from quantum physics and Einstein's theory of relativity.

THE EJACULATORY SCHOOL

This has been in existence for hundreds of years and will outlast Experimentalism, Birdyak and anything else the avant garde cares to invent.

Open any book of poetry and you will find small words of exhortation, amazement, shock or delight at the beginning of one line or another:

Oh how hideous it is... (Ezra Pound)

O fie upon the virgin beds... (Thomas Randolph)

Ah God! that it were possible... (Alfred, Lord Tennyson)

Say! You've struck a heap of trouble... (Robert W Service)

Gush! – flush the man, the being with it, sour or sweet...
(Gerard Manley Hopkins)

Ah, what avails the sceptred race!
Ah, what the form divine... (Walter Savage Landor)

O sylvan Wye! thou wanderer through the woods...
(William Wordsworth)

Alas! regardless of their doom
The little victims play! (Thomas Gray)

Some poets manage three ejaculations in one line:

O Peace, O Dove, O shape of the Holy Ghost
(Richard Watson Dixon)

But there are others who base their whole output on these (usually) monosyllabic openings:

But hark! the cry is Astur:
And lo! the ranks divide; (Thomas Babington Macaulay)

Dr Samuel Johnson began his 'An Epitaph upon the Celebrated Claudy Philips, Musician, who died very poor' as though about to admonish the poor deceased:

Philips!

JOHN BETJEMAN (1906-1984)

Betjeman used an enormous number of 'ohs', often at the beginnings of poems, but also broadened the Ejaculatory Vocabulary by including 'Huzza!', 'Look up!', 'Come on, come on', 'Hark!', 'Take me, Lieutenant!', 'Row like smoke!', 'Behold!', 'Swing up!', 'Swing down!', and some complete lines that only he could have written:

Come, friendly bombs and fall on Slough
Oh! full Surrey twilight! importunate band!
Oh! strongly adorable tennis-girl's hand!

Stop the trolley-bus, stop!

Early Electric! With what radiant hope
Men formed this many branched electrolier

Return, return to Ealing,
Worn poet of the farm!

Oh where's mid-on? And what is silly point?
Do six balls make an over? Help me, God!

THOMAS BABINGTON MACAULAY (1800-1859)

Macaulay relied heavily on 'O!' and 'Ho!' but was also a keen 'Hark!'-ist, and often took the precaution of starting a poem with 'Attend!', presumably conscious that his audience might well be about to go to sleep.

Ho! strike the flagstaff deep, Sir Knight: ho!
scatter flowers, fair maids:
Ho! gunners fire a loud salute: ho! gallants,
draw your blades.

Hark! Hark! – What means the trampling
of horsemen on our rear?

Lo, I will stand at thy right hand…

Point out that Macaulay's ejaculations are not in the same league as Betjeman's, being used merely to retain the metre of the line. For lo! it's trivial information of this kind that keeps the real expert at bay.

EDWARD FITZGERALD (1809-1883)

Fitzgerald's most famous poem, the translation of 'The Rubaiyat of Omar Khayyam of Naishapur', begins with even less optimism as to its reception than Macaulay had:

'Awake!'…

as though the audience, or possibly the reader, is already asleep. (If you think it's impossible to read poetry and be asleep at the same time, you've either never taught English Literature, or you've been very lucky, or you've never read anything from the eighteenth century.)

Fitzgerald, like Macaulay, was an 'O!' and 'Oh!' man, but, being more sensuous, he was also fond of 'Ah!', as though smacking his lips, or her bottom. As befits the author of 'The Rubaiyat', Fitzgerald had a full range of ejaculations:

Ah, my Beloved, fill the cup*…

Lo! some we loved…

Ah, make the most of what we yet may spend…

Fools! your Reward is neither Here nor There!

Oh, come with old Khayyam…

Ah, fill the cup*…

Oh, Thou, who didst with Pitfall and with Gin**…

Alas, that Spring should vanish with the Rose!

Ah, Moon of my Delight…

There are still people writing this sort of stuff today. You have been warned.

---

* Fitzgerald was also very fond of emptying the cup.

** Presumably this was what he liked to fill it with.

THE POPULAR SCHOOL

It is impossible to avoid poetry; it is almost as ubiquitous as dog mess, and just as nasty to step in. Even if you stay resolutely at home, shut in a darkened room, it will come thudding through your letter box in the form of greetings cards.

These verses represent Poetry for the Masses, the essence of which is the belief that trite sentiments are best immortalised in verse. Nobody would dream of translating the message of a greeting card into prose, but there are two mitigating circumstances:

1. Trying to find a new way of saying 'Happy Birthday' in verse is a bit like trying to find a new way of serving bangers and mash.

2. Writers of greetings card verses are working in the great tradition of the Poets Laureate – compiling verses for special occasions (or occasional verse as it is called on occasion).

Poet Laureate is the title given to a bard appointed by the UK government to write verse for occasions of national importance or significance. For his (or her, one should now also say, in light of Carol Ann Duffy's appointment as the first female Poet Laureate in 2009) great sin, they are given an annual stipend of a butt of sack (approximately 600 bottles of sherry – i.e., about a tenth of a poet's annual alcohol consumption) and charged with the duty of writing patriotic verse whenever the country does anything remotely embarrassing (diplomatic coup,

Royal birth, going to war, clinching a trade contract with Taiwan, winning a bronze medal at the Olympics).

One thing that really should be included in the annual stipend is a chalice (poisoned, you understand) from which to drink the sack, so tricky a job is the Laureateship. Over the years the Poet Laureate has kept a lower or higher profile as they have seen fit; Wordsworth, for example, wrote not a jot during his tenure. Recent postholder Andrew Motion, who wrote plenty in the role, has remarked: 'The day I stopped being Laureate, the poems that had been very few and far between came back to me'.

The main problem with the role, of course, is that poetry is jolly difficult to write to order; as a result, few laureates have ever written anything worthwhile. For example:

Across the wires the electric message came:
'He is no better: he is much the same.'

from a poem about Edward VII's illness written by Alfred Austin (appointed 1892).

A notable exception is Alfred, Lord Tennyson (appointed 1850), the longest holder of the post, who could even turn national disasters into such glories as:

Half a league, half a league,
Half a league onward.
All in the valley of Death
Rode the six hundred.
('Charge of the Light Brigade')

Bluffers should bone up on a few unknown ones, such as Nahum Tate (appointed 1692, died 1715) whose most famous poem was in praise of tea; Colley Cibber (appointed 1730, died 1757), an actor who also wrote plays of which playwright Congreve said, 'They have in them things that were like wit, but in reality were not wit'; and Thomas Wharton (appointed 1785, died 1790) who revived the sonnet and edited a book of verse called *The Oxford Sausage*.

WILLIAM TOPAZ McGONAGALL, POET AND TRAGEDIAN (1825-1902)

McGonagall is the world's finest bluffing poet ever, grossly and wickedly ignored until the 1950s. All his life this proud son of Dundee was the victim of hoaxes, practical jokes and leg-pulls, but his sublime muse rises above all this. Particular gems to look out for include the memorable trio of poems:

The Railway Bridge of the Silvery Tay

Beautiful Railway Bridge of the Silvery Tay
That has caused the Emperor of Brazil to leave
His home far away, incognito in his dress,
And view thee ere he passed along en route to Inverness...

The Tay Bridge Disaster

Beautiful Railway Bridge of the Silv'ry Tay!
Alas! I am very sorry to say
That ninety lives have been taken away
On the last Sabbath day of 1879
Which will be remember'd for a very long time...

and

An Address to the New Tay Bridge

Beautiful new railway bridge of the Silvery Tay...

AMERICAN POETRY AND SOME OF THE REST

I t's a good idea to make American poetry your bluffing speciality as there has been only 200 years of the stuff, if you discount the indigenous poetry of the Crow, Blackfeet, Apache, Sioux, etc.

The earliest recognisable poet from the USA was probably Anne Bradstreet (1612-1672), but the founding figures of American poetry are generally reckoned to be Ralph Waldo Emerson (1803-1882) and Edgar Allan Poe (most American poets have three names). In 1837, Emerson marched into Harvard University and delivered an address called 'The American Scholar', the message of which was that nature and instinct are better guides for human behaviour than books and learning. It didn't go down well at the time, but Oliver Wendell Holmes later called it 'Our Intellectual Declaration of Independence'.

EDGAR ALLAN POE (1809-1849)

James Russell Lowell (1819-1891) summed up Poe thus:

Here comes Poe with his Raven, like Barnaby Rudge,
Three fifths of him genius, two fifths sheer fudge.

Poe kept well away from long poems and from those that preached moral improvement. He also loathed Henry Wadsworth Longfellow's rhythmic storytelling (though 'Hiawatha' is almost certainly the best-known American poem in England).

Poe's poetical philosophy was simple:

Q. What is the most melancholy of topics?
A. Death.
Q. What is the most beautiful of topics?
A. A beautiful woman.
Q. What, therefore, is the best thing to write a poem about?
A. The death of a beautiful woman.

Poe wrote a lot along these lines.

WALT WHITMAN (1819-1892)

The most celebrated work of Walt Whitman is *Leaves of Grass* (or *Song of Myself* as it was called in its final edition), an extensive collection written over a period of many years. His poetry is proud, audacious and pioneering, and a lot of it is sexually outspoken, which made Whitman (Walter 'Walt' Whitman to give him the obligatory three names) very popular with other nineteenth-century poets (Rossetti, Swinburne) and very unpopular with everyone else. 'I am large, I contain multitudes', Whitman wrote in section 51 of the poem. Well, top marks for honesty at least.

EMILY DICKINSON (1830-1886)

Unlike most poets, who are desperate to see their work in print, only a handful or so of Emily Dickinson's poems were published before she died aged 55, leaving more than 1,700 poems. Recognition came late, about 70 years after her death; she is reckoned a genius by many. Dickinson adopted a one-club approach to punctuation, employing the long em-dash (—) in place of the full set of punctuation marks that might have been expected. Early editors of her work sought to remedy what they saw as a glaring fault but only managed to attenuate the force of her writing. Compare, for example, the doctored stanza:

The brain is wider than the sky,
For, put them side by side,
The one the other will include
With ease, and you beside

with the original:

The Brain—is wider than the Sky—
For—put them side by side—
The one the other will contain
With ease—and You—beside—

The former isn't a patch on the latter, largely because the em-dashes give the writing an energy and urgency which the standard punctuation manages to destroy. You can be enthusiastic about her poetry, calling it highly strung, lyrical, paradoxical, gnomic – but check first that you know what 'gnomic' means (*see* 'Glossary'). Dickinson led a quiet, and latterly reclusive, life which it is safe to assume did not involve the use of class-A drugs. Besides, she had no need of them, it seems, given the hit she got from a good shot of pure poetry: 'If I feel physically as if the top of my head were taken off, I know that is poetry', she said.

ROBERT FROST (1874-1963)

Robert Frost began writing poetry when he was in his late thirties (around 1912) and his early works have an archaic touch ('She talks and I am fain to list'). Later his poetry became more powerful and awarded him four Pulitzer Prizes and 44 honorary degrees.

Frost was a farmer (although perhaps not a very assiduous one) in New Hampshire and many of his poems reflect his chosen profession. His poetry has an easiness about it, being almost folksy at times. Powerfully direct:

Two roads diverged in a wood, and I—
I took the one less traveled by,
And that has made all the difference.
('The Road Not Taken')

universal in their reach:

The woods are lovely, dark and deep.
But I have promises to keep,
And miles to go before I sleep,
And miles to go before I sleep.
('Stopping by Woods on a Snowy Evening')

and, at times, shocking, as in this poem about a boy

working in a saw mill who dies after losing a hand:

They listened at his heart.
Little—less—nothing!—and that ended it.
No more to build on there. And they, since they
Were not the one dead, turned to their affairs.
('Out, Out—')

Frost's poetry has had a profound influence on many a twentieth-century poet. The poet whom he had most influence upon, however, wasn't even a poet when they met (i.e., a poet but he didn't know it). In 1912 Frost brought his family over the pond to live, and while in England he befriended the reviewer and biographer Edward Thomas. It was Frost who convinced Thomas to begin writing poetry, and we must be thankful that he did, for Thomas wrote more than 140 poems in the two years after he began, the sublime 'Adlestrop' being among them.

WILLIAM CARLOS WILLIAMS (1883-1963)

The happy thing about Williams is that he was a Cubist, Surrealist, Symbolist, Objectivist, Imagist, Lyricist poet, so you can say anything you like about him. His most famous poem is a skinny little thing called 'The Red Wheelbarrow'. Here it is in full:

so much depends
upon
a red wheel
barrow
glazed with rain

water
beside the white
chickens.

As with any poem, there are a range of responses available to this. 'If you say so, William,' being just one of them.

EZRA POUND (1885-1972)

Pound was dismissed from his first job as teacher of Romance languages at Wabash College, Indiana, on suspicion of moral turpitude and 'Bohemian behaviour' – you can make what you like of that – and his life was one long slide into the unacceptable. He left the USA and went to Italy, where he preached anti-Semitism and became a big hit on Italian radio during the Second World War. After the war he was tried for treason but found unfit to plead, and was confined in a mental institution. Released in 1958, he lived to the ripe old age of 87 and wrote hundreds of 'Cantos'.

If you favour Pound, try to 'let the images fall into your memory without questioning the reasonableness of each at the moment; so that, at the end, a total effect is produced' (an observation credited to TS Eliot). If not, take a firm stand and declare that better poets have been locked away in mental institutions with less cause.

Aside from his own poetry, Pound's greatest contribution to English letters was the editing job he did on the draft of TS Eliot's *The Waste Land*, reducing the length of the original by over half. It is, you may suggest with impunity, a pity perhaps that TS Eliot did not return the compliment and thin down 'The Cantos' a tad.

ALLEN GINSBERG (1926-1997)

Ginsberg once described his poetry as 'Angelical Ravings'. One-time hero of the Beat Generation, there's hardly a line that doesn't mention 'madness', 'fix', 'narcotic haze', 'undressing', 'drunk', etc. If you rave about Ginsberg, you're likely to be met with blank stares by anyone under 40. If anyone over 40 raves to you about Ginsberg, they've probably got a blank stare but for a totally different reason.

SYLVIA PLATH (1932-1963)

Plath wrote most of her poetry at four o'clock in the morning, which may account for the depression that most of it engenders. It is heavy stuff. Don't read it at four o'clock in the morning. If – no, when, as it will inevitably happen to you if you hang out in poetryland for any length of time – a young person (female, first year at university, reading English) tells you with great enthusiasm that her favourite poet is Sylvia Plath, you must a) give her your sympathy and b) make your excuses and leave. Absolutely do not mention, and definitely do not praise, the British poet Ted Hughes (aka 'The Devil Incarnate' to any Plathites) on account of their tempestuous marriage and her subsequent suicide. Of course, marrying a dour Yorkshireman with an enormous chin would drive most sensitive young women to the brink.

DOROTHY PARKER (1893-1967)

Parker approached death with delightful wit, as in 'Résumé':

Razors pain you;
Rivers are damp;
Acids stain you;
And drugs cause cramp.
Guns aren't lawful;
Nooses give;
Gas smells awful;
You might as well live.

And live she did. It took Dorothy 74 years to drink herself to death, which is slow going for a poet.

Other American poets you should know the names of include Robert Lowell (1917-1977), who wrote lots, mainly about himself ('confessional poetry' being a label applied to Lowell's poetry among others in the 1950s and 1960s), Elizabeth Bishop (1911-1979) and John Ashbery (1927-).

Buffs love Ashbery, mainly because he's so cutesy and ironic that no one knows what on earth he's going on about. He did say one sensible thing, however, calling Elizabeth Bishop 'a poet's poet's poet', a comment that speaks of the high regard in which Bishop is held by almost all poets in the universe. The good thing about Bishop is that you can familiarise yourself with her work fairly quickly because a) her poetic output was extremely slender (70 poems published in her lifetime in four slim volumes), b) it is accessible and c) it is simply the greatest poetry written in the twentieth century. If Rossetti, as suggested earlier, could reasonably be thought of as the most unhappy of English poets, Bishop may have some claim for the American title. 'When you write my epitaph you must say I was the loneliest person that ever lived', she wrote to Robert Lowell on one occasion – a claim which doesn't stand up to a lot of scrutiny when you consider that an edition of her collected letters runs to more than 500 pages. But poets – even the best – play fast and loose with the truth, especially if it might get them a bit of sympathy.

SONGWRITERS AS POETS

There's one way to approach American poetry without having to read any of it (always the preferred way of approaching poetry) and still appear an expert on the subject. Some of the slickest, liveliest and most moving verse from the USA is to be found in the lyrics of songs. The names to remember above all are Lorenz Hart (of Rodgers and Hart), EY Harburg and Ira Gershwin. Books of their work have been published, showing, in the case of Hart especially, a massive, sophisticated and witty output. The great advantage is that here is an immense volume of poetry that you already know. The great difficulty is managing to recite these poems without bursting into song. Claim that the appeal is in the 'wonderfully rhythmic quality of the verse' and in 'the innovative use of rhyme', e.g., Cole Porter's:

> ...flying too high/with some guy/in the sky/is my idea of nothing to do... ('I Get a Kick Out of You')

> While you love your lover let/blue skies be your coverlet... ('Mountain Greenery')

or the verse of Ira Gershwin's 'Our Love is Here to

Stay' written to the last song George Gershwin ever wrote
and in which Ira is mourning the death of a much-loved
brother. Avoid Oscar Hammerstein II.

The other American poets to try, without hurting your
brain, are ee cummings (the man with the broken caps
key) and Ogden Nash – author of the delightful ditties:

Shake, oh shake the ketchup bottle
None will come, and then a lottle.

And:

The cow is of the bovine ilk;
One end is moo, the other, milk.

Who ever said that American culture lacks depth?

AND THE REST...

This book purports to help the tyro rub shoulders with
the cognoscenti without coming a cropper in the process.
It doesn't set itself up to represent the whole of poetry in
English. However, it would leave the bluffer vulnerable and
exposed if it did not recommend that he or she familiarise
himself or herself somewhat with poetry written in English
from countries other than the UK and USA. Any history
of poetry – even a rollercoaster such as this one – needs
to stop and admire the poetry of great Irishmen such as
Yeats and Heaney; nor could it look itself in the mirror if
it did not mention the poetry coming out of Australia. Les
Murray is probably the most well-known – a large man who
writes large poems. There is a lot of Murray (and a lot of

it is worth reading) but it is certainly less time-consuming to get to know the work of an Australian rejoicing in the name of Kenneth Adolf Slessor (*see* 'The Lakes, the Patriots and the War Poets'), a journalist writing in the 1930s and 1940s whose entire output amounts to about 100 poems. 'You know, of course, that Murray was highly influenced by Slessor' is a sure-fire bluff; hardly anyone has heard of Slessor and you can therefore expose your interlocutor's ignorance of Aussie poetry without mercy.

Airy yet extremely knowing mention must be made also of the poetry of the Caribbean, of which Nobel Prize-winning Derek Walcott is perhaps the foremost exponent. 'Ah, "Omeros,"' you may opine, while hoisting a plagiaristic eyebrow, 'Walcott handles English with a closer understanding of its inner magic than most, if not any, of his contemporaries'; and silently thank Robert Graves for the accolade.

Remember that the slim volume all the critics are raving about today may be on the 'remaindered' pile tomorrow.

THE CURRENT STATE

Bluffers should remember that the slim volume all the critics are raving about today may be on the 'remaindered' pile tomorrow. Never commit yourself to reading every issue of every poetry magazine (there are lots in print and squillions online) or checking the poetry shelves of your local bookstore to make sure you haven't missed a new edition of *Poetry Review, Ambit* or *Magma Poetry*.

Let others sift through the bulging granaries of verse, sorting the less bad from the terrible. We are only now learning, or rather deciding, who were the good poets of the 1980s and 1990s, and the jury on poets of the noughties will be out for a good while yet.

Faced with an expert who is parading superior knowledge of contemporary poets, the best path for the bluffer is to be unstintingly admiring: 'You're reading all these new apprentices? How brave! I'm afraid it will take me the rest of my life to do justice to the late medieval mnemonics.' It's a pretty safe bet that the enthusiast won't know that by 'late medieval mnemonics' you mean 'Green Grow the Rushes, O'.

Like any other subject involving the acquisition and dissemination of vast quantities of knowledge, nobody can ever hope to know everything about poetry. But if you've got this far, and you've absorbed at least a modicum of the information and advice contained within these pages, then you will almost certainly know more than 99% of the rest of the human race about what poetry is and how you can pretend to know more about it than you do.

What you now do with this information is up to you, but here's a suggestion: be confident about your newfound knowledge, see how far it takes you, but above all have fun using it. You are now a bona fide expert in the art of bluffing about a rhythmic language of great beauty and emotional sincerity – especially in the hands of the great William Topaz McGonagall (unjustifiably derided as the worst poet in British history).

Think you're ready to shine with your knowledge of poetry? Test it first with our quiz at bluffers.com.

GLOSSARY

Anapest A dactyl (*see* below) flying backwards, e.g., *de-de dum*.

Aphorism Any short, pithy statement into which much thought or observation is compressed. Therefore very rare.

Ballad Simple poem of spirit in mercifully short verses and often easy to follow. Dates from the fifteenth century.

Blank verse Poetry written by poets too lazy to be bothered with rhymes, but who were good at counting up to 10. Invented by the Earl of Surrey (*see* 'Poets and Death').

Couplet Two lines of poetry, as in:

> *Auntie, did you hurt yourself, falling from that tree?*
> *Would you do it once again, please 'cos my friend here*
> *didn't see?* ('Ruthless Rhymes', Harry Graham)

Dactyl A metrical foot consisting of one long and two short syllables, e.g., *dum de-de*. Comes from the Greek for 'joints of the finger'.

Elegiac distich A couplet consisting of a hexameter and a pentameter:

> *dum de de, dum de de, dum de de, dum de de, dum de de, dum dum,*
> *dum dum, dum dum, dum dum, dum dum, dum dum.*

(It reads better if you use actual words.)

Elegy Not the sort of poem to cause a rash but a song of lamentation, often a funeral ode. You don't get many of them these days.

Elizabethan sonnet A rhyming scheme favoured by Shakespeare: abab/cdcd/efef/gg.

Gasometer Measurement of sincerity in poetry.

Gnomic Full of maxims (the slogans, not the machine guns). Sententious. Aphoristic.

Haiku Japanese verse consisting of three lines of five, seven and five syllables respectively. The most famous classical haiku writer was Basho.

Hexameter A line of six metrical feet, usually five dactyls and a spondee (*see* below), although you can have five spondees and one dactyl if you like – but never use a spondee on the fifth foot.

Iambic Lines based on iambuses, i.e., feet consisting of a short followed by a long syllable – *de dum*.

Iconoclastic What every poet would like to be – thumbing his or her nose at venerated images.

Jongleur Reciter of licentious and merry metrical tales. As a profession it has always lacked career prospects.

Lay A song sung by a minstrel.

Little Tich Music hall artist who wore two long feet or spondees.

Lyric Short poem divided into stanzas or strophes, directly expressing the poet's own thoughts and sentiments. The suggestion is that all other poetry doesn't, and is therefore cribbed.

Metre Any form of poetic rhythm: also, a unit of measurement that the British are still yards behind.

Minstrel Individual who used to wander about in medieval times singing his own and other people's verses. Now happily defunct.

Neo A term often misused. Strictly, it means 'new', but it's often used to mean 'a bit like…'

Ode Not as familiar in style as a song – more a rhymed lyric in the form of an address. All odes start 'O!', except those by Keats and Cyril Fletcher.

Panegyric Boot-licking.

Pentameter Five-foot line of verse. English heroic pentameters had 10 syllables – *dum dum dum dum dum dum dum dum dum dum* – and so were jolly *dull dull dull dull*…

Petrarchan sonnet A rhyming scheme invented by Petrarch who was a great fan of Swedish minstrels, hence: abba/abba, followed by two or three other rhymes in the remaining six lines of the sonnet.

Rhapsodes Ancient performers of poetry who very sensibly carried big sticks. Nowadays it's people who have to listen to poetry who should be armed.

Scansion The act of scanning a line of verse to detect its rhythm. The act of forcing English public schoolboys to scan poetry is single-handedly responsible for ensuring that whole generations were put off verse for life.

Slim volume Twee name given to a book of poetry. Books of contemporary poetry are kept slim because nobody really wants to read much contemporary poetry.

Sonnet A poem of 14 lines.

Spondee Metrical foot of two long syllables, e.g., *dum dum*.

Stanza A verse.

Strophe A complicated Greek metrical construction that usually went wildly wrong, hence 'catastrophe'.

Trochee The opposite of an iambus, e.g., *dum de*.

Troubadour Essentially a lyric poet from southern France, eastern Spain or northern Italy, who sang songs of chivalry and gallantry in the Provençal language. Most troubadours were taken to the pass of Roncesvalles to be wiped out.

BLUFFING NOTES

....
....
....
....
....
....
....
....
....
....
....
....
....
....
....
....
....
....
....
....
....
....
....
....
....
....
....

Bluffing Notes

....
....
....
....
....
....
....
....
....
....
....
....
....
....
....
....
....
....
....
....
....
....
....
....
....
....
....

Bluffing Notes

Bluffing Notes

....
....
....
....
....
....
....
....
....
....
....
....
....
....
....
....
....
....
....
....
....
....
....
....
....
....

Bluffing Notes

....
....
....
....
....
....
....
....
....
....
....
....
....
....
....
....
....
....
....
....
....
....
....
....
....
....
....

Bluffing Notes

Bluffing Notes

THE *Bluffer's*® GUIDE TO

THE HEADLINES

**SIGN UP FOR YOUR
FREE WEEKLY DIGEST AT
BLUFFERS.COM!**

Every Friday, receive our essential
news recap: a bluffer's must-have guide
to who did what and what happened
when during the week that was.

BLUFFERS.COM

**FOLLOW US ON TWITTER:
@BLUFFERSGUIDE**

**LIKE US ON FACEBOOK:
FACEBOOK.COM/BLUFFERSGUIDES**

NEW EDITIONS

Become an instant expert with these new and forthcoming Bluffer's Guides®.

BEER	OPERA
BOND	QUANTUM UNIVERSE
CARS	RACES
CHOCOLATE	ROCK MUSIC
CRICKET	RUGBY
CYCLING	SAILING
DOGS	SEX
FOOTBALL	SKIING
GOLF	SURFING
HIKING	TENNIS
INSIDER HOLLYWOOD	WINE
JAZZ	YOUR OWN BUSINESS
MANAGEMENT	

BLUFFERS.COM
@BLUFFERSGUIDE